Funny Polis and This and That as Observed by John the Hat

An environmentally friendly book printed and bound in England by
www.printondemand-worldwide.com

Mixed Sources
Product group from well-managed
forests, and other controlled sources
www.fsc.org Cert no. TT-COC-002641
© 1996 Forest Stewardship Council

FSC

PEFC Certified

This product is
from sustainably
managed forests
and controlled
sources

PEFC
PEFC/16-33-415

www.pefc.org

This book is made entirely of chain-of-custody materials

www.fast-print.net/store.php

FUNNY POLIS AND THIS AND THAT
AS OBSERVED BY JOHN THE HAT
Copyright © John the Hat 2014

A catalogue record for this book is available from the British Library

ISBN 978-178456-070-6

First published 2014 by
FASTPRINT PUBLISHING
Peterborough, England.

FUNNY POLIS AND THIS AND THAT
AS OBSERVED BY JOHN THE HAT

In The Beginning

I was born and brought up in the town of Blairgowrie, the raspberry and strawberry capital of the free world.

I had left school at fifteen and had dutifully served my time for five years as a plumber and heating engineer. I had also attended Dundee Trades College and had been awarded a First Class City and Guilds Diploma in that profession.

However, I had no intention of remaining in that employment after I had completed my five year apprenticeship. As my parents said, "You can do what you like now Johny, now that you have a trade to fall back on."

One reason I left was that, only too often, plumbers were called out to clear drains and cesspools of human and animal excrement. In particular dairy farm cesspools, and there were an awful lot of dairy farms around Blairgowrie.

The method for clearing both kinds of cesspool were the same; put on a pair of wellies and get into the pool. As you can imagine, the smell was indescribable, although nauseating comes close.

We normally worked in pairs with the apprentice (yes, that was me) shovelling human and animal excrement into a bucket which the labourer disposed of. In the case of the dairy farm cesspool, there were cowpats several feet deep and it covered about the same area as a modern Olympic standard swimming pool. Okay, I am prone to exaggerate at times, but they were large cesspools and it took a lot of shovelling to empty them.

Although I quite enjoyed fitting central heating systems, kitchens, bathrooms, etc., I had absolutely no intention of shovelling shit for the rest of my working life. I therefore looked around for alternative employment which I intended to pursue once I had completed my apprenticeship.

I finished my time at 12 noon on a Saturday and was now officially a time-served journeyman plumber and heating engineer. However, I never worked one day as a fully-fledged plumber because I started out at 9 a.m. on the Monday in my next profession as an insurance agent.

I much preferred going out to work in an immaculate suit, shirt and tie, driving around all over Perthshire, as my round covered most of that county. Although I was happy with the insurance company, after two years I was again getting restless and thinking about trying out another challenge.

I had mentioned to my family that I was thinking of trying something else. My mum said, "Why don't you join the police, Johny? You're a braw big lad and you will make a good policeman."

A few days later, I visited Dundee Police Office to make enquiries about joining. I told the large inspector at the front desk about my intentions.

He looked me up and down scornfully and stated, "You have to be six feet in your stocking soles to join this police force, wee man, so that rules you out." He looked at me thoughtfully for a few seconds, then added, "However, they take wee men of five foot ten down in Glasgow. Why don't you try them?"

I made enquiries with the City of Glasgow Police, filled in the appropriate application forms and thought no more of it.

Six weeks later, I was out dancing in Coupar Angus on a Saturday night. As usual, I had spent several hours with my mates boozing in the local pub before arriving at the dance hall to eye up the young ladies.

I saw one such lady home at the end of the evening. This meant that I had to walk the five miles back to Blairgowrie. I eventually arrived home after 5 a.m. and tumbled wearily into my bed. At 7 a.m. that Sunday morning, my mother opened my bedroom door and said, "There's someone here to see you, Johny."

I prised open my bleary, bloodshot eyes with great difficulty and tried to focus them on two hazy figures standing at the foot of my bed.

I suddenly realised with shock and horror that the figures were a police inspector and a sergeant in uniform. I frantically went over the events of Saturday night in my head, but I couldn't think of anything that I had done that would bring the police to my bedside at 7 a.m. on a Sunday morning.

The inspector then said, "I take it that you are John Robertson."

"Yes sir, I am," I replied, still wondering, "What the hell do they want me for?"

"Well then," he said. "We will give you five minutes to get dressed, then we will take you down to the police station with us."

"Why are you taking me there?" I stammered, which was unusual as I had never suffered from a stammer before.

He replied, "To sit your entrance examination for the City of Glasgow Police. You did apply, didn't you?"

"Oh no!" I thought. "Less than two hours sleep and still half cut from the night before." I could not have been less prepared for an exam if I had tried.

Five minutes later, I was sitting in the back of a police car and five minutes after that, I was sitting at a desk with an examination paper in front of me.

They did the exam strictly by the book, telling me that the exam would start in exactly five minutes and would finish in exactly two hours. They also advised me that if I required a toilet break, a police officer would escort me there and back again.

Despite my woeful lack of preparation, I somehow managed to pass the entrance exam. (I believe it was because I managed to spell my name correctly!) A short time later, I was instructed to attend the police training school in Oxford Street, Glasgow for a medical examination.

I arrived at the police training school, which was my first ever visit to Glasgow. Talk about the country bumpkin coming to the city. The sergeant in charge immediately instructed me to remove my shoes. He then proceeded to measure my height. He pulled a rod down on top of my head and stared intently at it.

"I make that five foot nine and seven eighths. No, just a second," he said as I stretched every muscle and sinew upwards, "I make that five foot ten inches exactly."

That was the critical part passed, as I sailed through the physical fitness examination with nonchalant ease. I was a fit, athletic young man in those days.

Six weeks later, I trundled to a halt outside the police training school in a huge articulated lorry (my father was a long distance lorry driver and was passing through Glasgow that morning).

I jumped out of the lorry, suitcase in hand, to begin my police career. Two weeks at the police training school, followed by six weeks at Tulliallan Police College, then a further two weeks back at the police training school and we were ready for life out on the beat.

My first experience of beat patrol consisted of two hours with an older and experienced officer, much to their dismay as they didn't much care to babysit a brand new rookie probationary constable.

I made my way to Partick Police Office for my first night on patrol in a double decker bus. I had no idea where it was and had to ask another passenger where I should get off the bus for the police station. He looked at me incredulously and said, "Haw, big man, we're supposed to ask you for directions, no the ither way aboot." However, he then told me exactly where to alight.

At least I had the satisfaction of having left Dundee as a wee man, and now here I was in Glasgow being acknowledged as a big man.

The following selection of hopefully amusing stories and anecdotes did take place more or less as described, although to spare my colleagues blushes, the names have all been changed.

John the Hat

S ince the autumn of 1963, I have been known to all of my colleagues as John the Hat.

Even now, well over forty years later, if I meet an old colleague, the greeting I receive is invariably the same.

"It's John the Hat. How are you doing, Hat? How are things with you?"

Most of them don't know how I received that particular nickname and many of them have asked me how I came to be called John the Hat. I always tapped the side of my nose and answered, "That's for me to know."

However, it's time to spill the beans and explain the facts and circumstances, which are quite comical and embarrassing.

All probationary constables started with a month at Tulliallan Police College before joining up with the division allocated to them within Glasgow. I joined up with the City of Glasgow Police some years before it became part of Strathclyde Police Force.

At that time, a brand new fresh-faced young probationary constable always started on night shift. This was in order to break them in gently, as there was much less of the public out and about during the night. There were strict regulations that a probationer must be accompanied at all times by an experienced officer until he had at least one year's service on the beat.

However, like all strict rules, there can be exceptional circumstances when even the strictest can be bent a little. On this particular night, I was on duty with an experienced officer on the Glasgow University beat. This beat covered the area of the University and the curry capital of Glasgow in Gibson Street and Bank Street, boasting a huge array of Indian and Chinese restaurants.

There had been a number of housebreakings taking place during the night in this area. It was therefore decided that my neighbour and myself would have separate refreshment breaks. I would have mine from 2 a.m. until 3 a.m. and his was from 3 a.m. until 4 a.m.

The thinking strategy behind this was that a uniformed presence on the streets might deter a would-be housebreaker. I was so raw and inexperienced that they would have had the same success dressing up a monkey in a police uniform.

Nevertheless, at 3 a.m. I was out on beat patrol on my own for the very first time. I was walking up Gibson Street with my police issue torch in my hand when it happened. I had just passed Tenement Close when I heard what sounded like two men coming down the stairs, walking out of the Close behind me.

I didn't want to turn round and check them out, so I slowed down to allow them to pass. This was so that I could assess whether or not there was anything suspicious about them. After all, it was now 3.30 a.m. in the morning.

Just as the two men were passing me, my police hat was flicked off my head and landed on the roadway several yards away from me. I was completely amazed and astonished at the bare-faced cheek and effrontery of the two men and spun round to face them.

I was mightily relieved to see that it was two of my shift colleagues on their night off, returning from a late night party.

However, my relief didn't last very long as Tommy and Stewart, two jovial pranksters who loved playing practical jokes, ran over to my hat and booted it further up Gibson Street.

Luckily for me, there were no members of the public around to witness my embarrassment and mortification. Every time I bent over to pick it up, they managed to kick it away from me. It must have looked like an episode from a Carry On film.

Eventually, I managed to retrieve my hat, but it was now in a very sad and damaged condition. The black and white diced band around it had been ripped off and had gone sailing into the night sky. My new headpiece now looked like a bus driver's hat, albeit an extremely battered and misshapen one.

Tommy and Stewart were laughing uproariously. They thought that the whole thing was absolutely hilarious. On reflection, it probably was, although I didn't see the funny side of it at that particular time.

Luckily for me, every probationer is issued with two police hats. I had another one in my digs. Fortunately, it was only a short walk from our beat.

I was able to change hats and be back on patrol, looking brand new before my neighbour returned from his meal break. He asked me if I had been all right in his absence. I replied, "Of course. It's been absolutely quiet with nothing to report."

We now press the fast forward button to some four weeks later.

I had now completed my night shift duties and was on late shift. It was Saturday night and I had been invited to a party after we had finished.

As soon as our shift was over, it was straight to my digs to get changed out of my uniform and on with the party clothes. I then met up with my two good friends, yes, you've guessed it, Tommy and Stewart, (I don't hold a grudge) and off to the party we went, holding sizeable carryouts.

The party lasted all night and well into Sunday morning. We then left for a couple of hours kip at Tommy's digs before reporting back for duty on Sunday late shift. There was always a nominated senior officer on Sunday late shift duty, normally the superintendent or the chief superintendent.

The senior officer always attended a police office at 13.45 hours and carried out a uniform parade inspection. He checked out that trousers were neatly pressed, boots highly polished, short hair tidy and that we were all turned out in immaculate, pristine fashion. We had all been advised that the parade was to take place in Cranstonhill Police Office that day.

Tommy changed into his uniform, then we headed off to my digs where I did likewise. It was only at that stage that we realised with a jolt of alarm that we were running very late.

I pulled off my civvies, (civilian clothing) throwing them on my bed, and pulled on my uniform as quickly as I possibly could. Tommy was getting very anxious about the time and was berating me to hurry up.

It was like a sketch out of Francie and Josie with Tommy shouting, "Hurry up, hurry up, hurry up," and me replying, "Sure, Tommy, sure, Tommy, sure, I'm hurrying up as fast as I can."

I stuck on my hat and fastened my tunic buttons as we ran down the stairs. We then had to run all the way from my digs to Cranstonhill Police Office.

We bolted into the building virtually thirty seconds before the chief superintendent marched in and shouted out, "Attention all officers on parade"

We all leapt to our feet and stood to attention for the chief super to inspect us. All of my shift had appeared happy to see me that day, smiling broadly at me with two of them even remarking, "You are looking well today, John."

I was feeling quite confident; even a little smug about the inspection. After all, I had pressed my trousers, polished my boots and had even had a haircut the previous day. I was expecting a compliment about my appearance such as, "Very well turned out, officer."

Therefore, it came as a complete shock when the chief superintendent walked straight over to me. He was practically leaping in the air with rage and was obviously extremely irate and angry. He barked out at me,

"Probationary Constable Robertson! Who on earth do you think you are?"

Quick as a flash, Stewart shouted out, "John the Hat."

The entire shift then went into convulsions of hysterical laughter, except of course for the chief superintendent and me. He snapped at me, "Go take a look at yourself in the mirror, young man!"

I walked over to the full-length mirror, wondering what I could have possibly done to make him so angry. I looked at my reflection and to my horror and mortification saw that I was wearing the battered, misshapen bus driver's hat. In my haste to make the inspection in time, I had shoved on the wrong hat.

Tommy had of course spotted my error in my digs, but predictably had decided to say nothing and give the shift a good laugh. Oh, to be so lucky as to have friends like Tommy and Stewart.

The chief superintendent then instructed the Land Rover crew to conceal me in the rear of the vehicle, making sure that members of the public did not see me before I had changed into my new hat, and at least looked like a police officer.

From that day onwards, I was known throughout the force as John the Hat.

Over the years, I picked up another three nicknames. The first one was when I delivered a baby during my probationary period. I was naturally called John the Midwife for a short time.

The second one was earned on night shift in deepest winter. The frost was so thick it resembled snow. I had made a bad choice of uniform dress that night. I was wearing my thin plastic raincoat when I should have chosen my thick woollen great coat.

Consequently, I was chittering with the cold by 6 a.m. as I made my way to Ron's home bakery after diligently checking my beat.

I was really looking forward to hot rolls and large mugs of tea. I walked into the back of the bakery with my neighbour Mister Magoo. I walked over to the huge oven and stood with my back to it, gratefully thawing out.

I should explain why my good friend Alex had received that particular nickname. He was the first officer to join our police division after the rules had been relaxed to allow entrants who required to wear spectacles on a full-time basis to join the police. At that time there was a cartoon character featuring a very short sighted man called Mr Magoo. In those days most cops received a nickname and Alex being the first full-time spectacle user was an obvious candidate for that nickname.

I was chatting to Ron the baker when I smelled something burning. I quickly remarked, "You had better be careful. I think you are burning something."

Ron replied, "I don't think so John, I think it is you who is burning."

I turned around quickly and saw that my plastic raincoat had been touching the oven, had stuck to it and had actually melted off my back. Of course, Mister Magoo, Ron, his son and his wife thought that this was hilarious and were in fits of laughter about it.

At this time, the entire shift at Partick Police Office was to be dismissed and go off duty. I had asked Magoo to say nothing to spare my embarrassment, which he had agreed to do. Needless to say, once inside the police office, Magoo gleefully recounted the exact circumstances of my unfortunate accident to the entire shift, which of course had all of my colleagues in fits of laughter. For a short time after that I was known as Melting John. I wasn't exactly having much luck with police issue uniform equipment.

My next nickname came during the seventies. I was transferred from uniform to plainclothes duty for several years (perhaps they were cutting down their expenses in replacing my uniform).

My regular neighbour on plainclothes was my very good friend Willie who sadly is no longer with us and is greatly missed.

We were named after two fictitious detectives on a current television series at that time. I can hear you saying, "It was Regan and Carter from the Sweeney or it was Bodie and Doyle from the Professionals, or maybe even Starsky and Hutch."

It was none of them. It was in fact Charley Farley and Piggy Malone from the Two Ronnies series.

The criminal underworld in Partick must have been quaking in their boots at the thought of Charley Farley and Piggy Malone on their case.

However, all of those nicknames ran their course while John the Hat remains a permanent fixture. Ah well. Everything changes and everything remains the same.

I dare say when I meet Saint Peter at the Pearly Gates, he will say, "Ah, it's John the Hat. Come right in, Hat. We've been expecting you."

Break-In at Twenty-Two Storeys

It was a bitterly cold winter's night with a ferocious gale-force wind blowing. Jimmy the beat man was out patrolling in Scotstoun. His chinstrap was firmly secured to prevent his hat being whisked off his head and flying off into the night sky.

He received a call to attend at a tower block of flats on his beat. The gist of the call was that an elderly lady residing on the twenty-second floor was reporting an attempted housebreaking in progress.

This in itself was not unusual, but according to her, the housebreaker was trying to gain entry into the flat from the tiny balcony off her living room.

Now, as you can imagine, twenty-two floors is an exceedingly long way up, with no access onto this balcony except for the veranda doors in her living room.

Therefore, Jimmy quite reasonably presumed that the gale was making the doors creak and move, thus frightening the old lady. "Ah well," he thought. "At least I will get out of this freezing gale for a short time, and there is probably a cup of tea in it for me."

Luckily for Jimmy, the lifts were working, as he was dreading walking up twenty-two flights of stairs. He arrived at the flat and was taken straight into the living room. The old lady thanked him for coming and told him that someone was definitely trying to break in.

Jimmy thought to himself, "It is absolutely impossible for anyone to be on her balcony so many floors up, but I'd better pretend to take her complaint seriously."

"Certainly my dear, I will deal with the matter right away," he said, going through the motions for the old lady's benefit.

He then walked over to the glass doors and pulled back the curtains to look out onto the balcony. Unfortunately, the doors had not been opened for many years, and had been painted and repainted so many times that a solid joint had formed between the metal doors, not too dissimilar to a welded joint.

There was no way he could open the doors without using a hammer and chisel on the solid mass of paint. To make matters worse, dust and dirt over the years had covered the outside of the doors, making it totally impossible to see through to the balcony.

Jimmy tried to reassure the old lady, saying, "I'm absolutely positive that there isn't anyone on your balcony. I'm sure it's just the storm that you have been hearing." He went on to ask if she would like a cup of tea and offered to sit with her for a while, just to make sure there was not a problem.

The old lady retorted, "You think I'm dolly dimple and senile. You are just trying to humour me, aren't you son?"

In actual fact, it was exactly what Jimmy was thinking, but he replied, "Of course not madam. I wouldn't dream of it."

The old lady reiterated, "There is definitely a man on my balcony trying to break in."

Jimmy replied, "Of course there is madam and I'm sure that I will hear him shortly." He was actually thinking, "Aye, that will be right. After all, we are twenty-two storeys up a tower block."

Then it happened. Jimmy heard a loud groan coming from her balcony. He nearly fainted, as all along he had been totally convinced that it was a mixture of noises from the high winds and the old lady's imagination.

"I told you that there was a man on my balcony," said the old lady triumphantly. "You thought I was a senile old fool and you wouldn't believe me, would you, son?"

"Yes madam, it would appear that you were correct," Jimmy said as he heard more moans and groans. He then used a screwdriver and hammer to chip the paint off the metal doors and eventually managed to force them open for the first time in many years.

There on the balcony, moaning and groaning, lay an old man, but how on earth had he arrived on a balcony so high up?

It turned out that the old man resided on the twenty-third floor. He had decided that night that he had seen enough of this world and chose to commit suicide by jumping off his balcony.

Unfortunately, or should I say fortunately for him, when he made his jump, a huge gust of wind blew him back against the building and onto the old lady's balcony.

However, all's well that ends well. The old man decided after his miraculous escape that God was not ready for him yet and that he would enjoy the rest of his life until it was his time.

As for Jimmy, he decided that he would approach every call with an open mind in the future and would rule no situation out, regardless of how unlikely it appeared.

Making a Clean Breast of It

I t was a glorious Friday evening in mid summer and I was on late shift duty. I was the brand new probationary constable in our shift and still a raw young bumpkin from the berry fields of Blairgowrie. I was detailed to serve as the observer in the police Land Rover patrol vehicle, along with the regular driver.

The two police officers who were the regular crew of the vehicle were well known as jokers and wind-up merchants. However, one of them was off duty that day and being the boy (youngest probationer) of the shift, I was filling in for him.

The Land Rover was an excellent police patrol vehicle, as it had room in the rear for several prisoners. It often accommodated persons deemed to be drunk and incapable.

They were normally horizontal drunks, usually men, but occasionally women who were flat out from the effects of too much alcohol. They were lifted bodily and placed on the floor of the vehicle. It was almost physically impossible to manoeuvre a full-blown drunk into the back of an ordinary police car. Invariably, if it was accomplished, it was highly likely they would be sick all over the inside of the car.

If this happened in the back of a Land Rover it was simply hosed down in the police yard, then sent straight back out on patrol again. It was a very useful and versatile police vehicle indeed.

Anyway, back to the evening in question, we were patrolling the Charing Cross area at that time. In the early sixties there was (and probably still is) a large area from Blythswood Square, Anderston Cross and Charing Cross populated by the ladies of the night, or street prostitutes as they were known.

On the whole they were left to their own devices by the police. However, they all had to take their turn at being arrested for importuning in a public place, appearing at Glasgow District Court, just off Glasgow Cross. They were then fined by the Glasgow Stipendiary Magistrates and warned that they faced a term of imprisonment if they ever dared to appear before them again.

The ladies then looked suitably ashamed and contrite, vowing never to do it again. Of course, they all knew full well that they would be back out on the streets again that very same evening.

At times they were very useful to the police, often supplying information regarding serious crimes, as they saw and heard everything happening on the streets around them.

We were driving along a lane behind Charing Cross when we observed a large woman who was very obviously a lady of the night.

She was wearing a crop top, mini skirt and high-heeled boots. It was about 9.30 p.m., but still broad daylight with the sun beating down from a brilliant blue sky.

The Land Rover driver stopped the vehicle beside her. He greeted her as follows. "Hullaw rerr Big Annie. How's it gaun the night?" He was a Glaswegian, as was Big Annie who replied, "No bad. I've been getting a wee turn wie it bein a nice night."

My colleague then remarked, "This is John. He is the new boy in the shift." Unknown to me, he obviously winked or signalled to her, as she immediately walked round to my side of the Land Rover.

Both windows were fully open on this beautiful summer's evening. "How's it gaun John?" she said. "How do you like bein in Glesca Polis?"

I was a bit nonplussed and stammered nervously, "Oh, I'm quite enjoying it, thanks."

Then without any warning a large, pendulous, naked female breast was thrown in the window and quivered as it dangled in front of my incredulous eyes. It was about the size and shape of an outsized melon. I was completely shocked and stunned.

Big Annie was obviously highly amused at the amazed expression on my face and said, "How does that suit you son? Would that do you?"

I gulped nervously and replied, "Oh no, madam. There is far too much there for me. I could never manage all that."

Big Annie and my colleague then laughed uproariously at my embarrassment as she swiftly replaced her large appendage under her top.

I later learned that this trick was pulled on all the brand new probationers on their first duty as observer in the Land Rover. Needless to say I was the butt of all the jokes when we attended at the police office for our refreshment break.

However, time moves on and three months later, a brand new probationer started and I was no longer the boy of the shift.

Incidentally, in case you are wondering, did I do the right thing and warn the new boy to spare his blushes and mortification?

"DID I HELL!"

The Ryvita Diet

B ig Jim was the office beat man at Cranstonhill Police Office in the early sixties. He was called Big Jim not because of his height, but due to his truly impressive girth and width.

Jim had patrolled the beat for many years in the Cranstonhill area and knew all of the shopkeepers, restaurant and hotel managers, fish and chip and curry shop owners, etc. He was extremely popular with all of them, and to use an old Scottish expression, HE WOULD GET A PIECE AT ANYONE'S DOOR.

In those far off days, the local beat man was treated like royalty by the local traders and everything was free gratis and on the house.

Big Jim was extremely polite and would not refuse an offer of food or drink, as he felt that it was bad manners to do so. However, unfortunately for Jim his excessive good manners finally caught up with him and he suffered a heart attack.

Luckily for him it was relatively minor and he made a good recovery, but alas, the police doctor refused to sign him off to resume on full police duties. In fact, he wanted to pension him off on an ill health police pension.

Unfortunately for Jim he was several months short of twenty-six and a half years police service, which was the minimum service to attain a full thirty year pension. Being signed off for ill health and retiring early meant that Big Jim would lose a considerable amount of his pension.

After much humming and hawing and gnashing of teeth, the force doctor agreed to let Jim return to work, as long as it was only light duties indoors and not outdoors on normal beat duty.

Big Jim then resumed on indoor uniform bar duties at Cranstonhill Police Office, which meant that he would now qualify for a full police pension.

Big Jim's wife had received quite a fright over his heart attack and watched over him like a mother hen. She was very aware of the cause of his attack; mainly consumption of too much fatty food and carrying far too much weight. Therefore, she sent him out to work every day with a packed lunch.

She tried her best to give him a healthy low fat diet. This comprised of two Ryvita biscuits with cucumber, lettuce, tomato and cottage cheese.

Give Big Jim his due, he did try. For his first week back on shifts he dutifully munched his way through his Ryvita biscuits.

However, after one week Jim stated that he could eat no more cardboard sandwiches and that he was going back to proper food. Every day a different beat man was instructed to visit Jim's old friends and purchase something tasty for his meal break. Needless to say, although money was offered, none of Jim's old friends would even consider accepting payment for anything. They all said almost the same thing. "Give Big Jim our best wishes and I hope he enjoys his meal."

During Jim's enforced time off work after his heart attack he had actually lost a bit of weight, as his caring wife had been careful with the quality and quantity of the healthy home-cooked meals she prepared for him.

Therefore, Big Jim only got away with it for a few weeks before his concerned and dutiful wife noticed that her husband was putting on weight at an alarming rate, despite his extreme low fat Ryvita diet.

She challenged Jim about his weight gain and asked him for an explanation. Big Jim was a wily old cop and replied that it was because he was sitting at a desk all day and not walking the many miles he normally covered when out pounding the beat. He explained that it was simply the lack of exercise that was causing the weight gain.

However, luckily for Jim's health, his wife did not believe a second of his story. She telephoned the desk sergeant on Jim's shift and asked him what was going on. As it happened, the sergeant was also getting worried that Big Jim might eat himself into an early grave. He then worked out a plan with Jim's wife.

The following evening, Jim entered the refreshment room for his meal break. As usual, he offered his two Ryvita biscuits to anyone who fancied them. Strangely enough, his offer was seldom taken up.

Big Jim spread out his meal in front of him. It consisted of a fish supper accompanied by a pie, a white pudding and pickled onions to be washed down with a bottle of Irn Brew.

He gazed lovingly at his food and lifted his knife and fork to begin his large repast. At that precise moment his irate wife burst in through the door and caught him in the act. The indoor sergeant had timed it perfectly, keeping Jim's wife out of sight until he was just about to begin his meal.

There was much gnashing of teeth from Jim's wife and even the cunning old fox could not get out of this one, although he did try. He looked beseechingly around the room and said, "This is no my meal. Tell my wife who it belongs to." Every cop in the room said, "Well, it's certainly no mine. Keep me out of it."

A severely chastened and embarrassed Big Jim was forced back on his Ryvita diet, but this story has a happy ending. He realised that both his wife and his sergeant were acting in his best interests and were simply trying to keep him healthy.

He managed to complete his full police service on indoor duties and received his full pension when he retired, albeit more of a Slim Jim than a Big Jim.

Home Delivery

T his momentous event occurred when I had
completed about nine month's service as a
probationary constable.

I had just reached the point when I could be trusted to
perform beat duties on my own, although I still had some
fifteen months left before my probationary period was
completed.

On this particular evening I was on late shift from 2
p.m. until 11 p.m. I was nearing the end of my shift,
feeling quite confident, perhaps even a little smug. After
all, I had dealt with several calls with cool professionalism.

It was about 10.50 p.m. and I was about five minutes
walk from the police box. At this time our only
communication was via this method. There were no
personal radios in those far off days.

At that time, the procedure for officers going off duty
at the conclusion of a shift, was that they attended the
main police box on their beat and phoned themselves off
to the police switchboard.

I was therefore strolling nonchalantly and leisurely
towards the police box at 11 p.m., thinking to myself, "Job
done. That will do nicely." (Just how wrong could I
possibly be?)

Just then, a young man rushed out of a tenement close in Argyle Street, looking around frantically. Then he saw me and raced over shouting, "Thank God, it's the polis. Ah'm I glad to see you?"

I, on the other hand, was not nearly so glad to see him, as he was in a flat spin, panicking about something. I had that sinking feeling that I was not going to like what he was about to tell me, and boy, was I right about that?

He began babbling incoherently, the words tumbling out of his mouth, saying something about the wean's coming. I told him to slow down and asked, "What wean's coming?" He answered me, "Mah wean's coming. You'll need to hurry up."

I then asked him, "Where is the wean coming from?" He shouted back at me, "Where do you think the wean is coming from? Fae my wife's belly of course. She's in labour and she is huvvin the wean right noo."

The penny finally dropped and I understood why he was in such a blind panic. Oh no-o-o-o, my first night on the beat without a more senior cop with me and I was about to deliver a baby on my own.

I, of course maintained my composure and tried to look cool, unflappable and professional (if only). I asked the highly agitated young man if there was a midwife standing by.

"Oh, aye," he replied. "She is just waiting for me to phone her."

Taking control of the situation, I told him, "Then run to the telephone box (practically nobody had a house telephone back then) and tell her that it is extremely urgent that she attends immediately. I will go straight to your wife and assist her with the birth. Don't worry. We are fully trained to handle emergency childbirth."

"Oh, thank God," he exclaimed, swallowing my outrageous whopper of a lie hook, line and sinker. "I'll just go and phone the midwife then." With that, he ran off shouting, "It's the top flat, by the way. The door is open."

Full of trepidation, I made my way up the stairs, saw the open door and walked in, spotting a young lady lying on the settee in the living room, very obviously in the deepest throes of labour. Accompanying her was an older lady who was running about the room like a headless chicken.

She observed me and shouted, "It's all right now Aggie. The polis have arrived and will take care of everything." (Ah, such confidence in the polis. I only wished I shared her faith, as I was absolutely petrified!)

The older lady then said, "What can I do to assist you officer?" Thinking quickly, I replied, "Please fill up all the kettles and pots you can find and heat me up as much hot water as possible." I had no idea what I wanted all the hot water for, but I had heard people saying that in films featuring emergency births.

She obviously thought that I knew what I was doing, as she scurried away saying, "Yes officer. Right away officer. I then very nervously approached the young lady in full-blown labour.

She was extremely agitated and shouted at me, "For God's sake, do something. I'm ready for passing out."

My immediate thought was, "Aye, you and me both." However, I tried to at least appear cool and professional and replied "Of course madam. I will now see to the delivery of your baby."

I looked down to see the baby's head already beginning to emerge. "Take deep breaths and push madam." I instructed her. She retorted, "What the hell do you think I've been doing for the past hour."

I managed to get my hand under the baby's head and began easing it out. Once the head came out, the rest of its body emerged fairly quickly.

By this time, the other lady had reappeared from the kitchen and saw the newly born child. She immediately began shouting, "Oh, ya beauty. A baby boy. Just what they wanted."

I asked her to bring me some warm water and a sponge. I then cleaned the baby up, making sure that his mouth and nose were clear. Luckily for me, the baby began crying right on cue. I hadn't been looking forward to giving his bottom a wee slap.

To be absolutely fair, the baby and his mum had done all of the work with only the tiniest amount of assistance from me. Yet here were the two ladies praising me to the heavens with comments like, "A doctor or a midwife could not have delivered a baby as professionally as you did," and, "I will just send for you when I am having my next baby."

I basked in the totally undeserved praise for a few seconds, then stated, "It's all in the training at the police college. The standard is very high, don't you know?"

"Oh that's good," said the new mum. "Then I take it you will be cutting the cord now."

Oh no, I hadn't even thought about that. I broke out in a cold sweat; me and my big mouth. What could I do?

Sparring for time, I stated, "I'm sorry madam, but the uterus is still too dilated to safely cut the cord." (Where that came from I have no idea, I was waffling pure gobbledygook!)

However, once again, luck was with me as they both accepted my tall tale, with the older lady even saying, "The officer knows exactly what he is doing." (Aye, right, so he does.)

A few minutes later, they again suggested that it must be about time for cutting the cord.

"Yes, of course ladies," I replied. "I do believe so." At that very moment, the door opened and in came the husband accompanied by the midwife. (Hallelujah! Luck was still with me.)

I was almost ecstatic with relief and immediately relaxed. "Nice of you to arrive after the works all done," I quipped to the midwife. "I've left it for you to do the honours and cut the cord."

The midwife caught on immediately. She must have seen the look of pure unadulterated relief when I saw her arriving. She replied, "Thank you officer. That was kind of you to leave me something to do." She accompanied this with a knowing wink, obviously realising that I was floundering miles out of my depth.

I then made my way to the police box to phone myself off duty. There waiting for me was the shift inspector and the sergeant, as I was now considerably late. They were obviously ready to give me hell.

However, I quickly explained to them the relevant circumstances and why it had been totally impossible to advise them that I was engaged in an emergency situation. Once they realised that I had safely delivered a baby and that the mother and baby were both well, they completely changed their attitudes.

They then congratulated me on my handling of the birth in such a competent and professional manner (it would appear that sometimes you can fool all of the people all of the time).

If only they knew that I had been absolutely petrified the whole time. Cool and composed on the outside, like a swan floating on water, but paddling furiously under the surface.

This incident occurred when I had less than one year's police service. I went on to complete thirty-two years without another emergency birth on my watch. To say that I was happy and relieved about that is a considerable understatement.

The Docks

In the early sixties, the docks area of Glasgow was a booming, bustling hive of activity, with all kinds of merchant ships arriving from, and departing for, every corner of the world. The ships brought in all kinds of produce from their countries of origin and normally left with their holds crammed full of thousands of cases of the finest Scotch whisky.

Partick Police Station was known as the Marine Police Station, and our division was known as the Marine Division. This was because the entire southern divisional boundary was the exact centre of the River Clyde.

The workforce within the various docks on both sides of the Clyde were known simply as "The Dockers". They were a truly unique workforce, consisting of a large group of families who worked together as a team. Those jobs had been handed down from generation to generation. If your father and grandfather had not been dockers, then your chances of becoming one were well and truly non-existent. The sole criteria for becoming a docker was that you were born into it.

I cannot begin to imagine what our present P.C. brigade would make of this closed doors system of obtaining employment. However, in the early sixties, the system worked very well. The dockers were a clever, resourceful group of men who could probably have worked in any occupation.

Our remit as police officers was to keep theft from the docks down to a minimum; particularly theft of the many brands of excellent Scotch whisky, exported mainly for the American market. However, achieving this objective was as successful as King Canute ordering the tide not to come in. The "Dock Men" (as the cops performing this duty were known) did their best, but it was an impossible task.

The dockers were supremely well-organised and knew exactly where the dock cops were every minute of every day. They had their own tic tac system down to a fine art with almost imperceptible movements of their heads or hands.

The dockers were of the opinion that not all of the superb brands of export only Scotch whisky should be consumed by Americans. The method used to receive what they considered to be their legitimate share, was simple but highly effective. They all carried in their pockets a Stanley knife and a large roll of Sellotape. This was for the perfectly proper reason that they had to cut string when opening containers and seal insecurely packaged containers when loading or unloading from ships.

In literally seconds, the dockers were able to remove a bottle of whisky from a carton. They would cut along the top and down one side of the rear of the cardboard carton, open the flap, remove the whisky, then reseal it again with Sellotape. This was done with the speed, skill and precision of a surgeon, and could even be achieved with the dock police in close proximity. This was known as Plan A.

We knew how they did it, why they did it and when they did it, but with their superlative system of tic tac, it was impossible to actually catch them in the act of doing it.

On the odd occasion when there was only one gang of dockers loading a whisky boat and the dock police were able to devote their full undivided attention and stand over them, they had another cunning plan to outwit us.

They would then revert to Plan B. That is, they would have an accident, (well, they always claimed it was an accident) and we couldn't possibly disprove that it wasn't, could we? How on earth could we possibly suggest or infer that the accidents were staged or rigged?

The dockers would load a pallet with dozens of cardboard cartons of whisky. They would instruct the crane driver to lift the pallet up from the side of the dock and deposit it onto the deck of the ship. There, another gang of dockers unloaded the pallet and packed the containers of whisky into the hold of the ship.

Towards the end of their shift when the dock police had been particularly vigilant in their surveillance and had managed to prevent plan A being used, they would revert to Plan B which went like this. The loaded pallet would be lifted about twenty feet up. The crane driver would then jerk the lever, causing one or two cartons to come crashing down to the ground, smashing most of the bottles contained therein.

The dockers would pick up their bucket which was kept close beside them and was always kept in pristine condition for such eventualities. They would then pour the whisky from the cardboard containers into the bucket to be divided up at the end of their shift.

One bonus for all the dock personnel, e.g. harbour masters, tug boat pilots and crew, various tradesmen, etc. was the finders keepers policy operated within the docks. The modus operandi (method used) of the dockers after removing the bottles from the cartons was to conceal them in various ingenious hiding places to be collected later.

Very often, their plank (as their ill-gotten gains were referred to) were found by the aforementioned dock personnel. It was impossible to return the bottles to the expertly sealed cartons, for they were either loaded onto the ship or in most occasions already out on the high seas.

Even the companies exporting the whisky did not want to know. Their position was that their cargo of whisky had been counted, checked and verified when loaded onto the ship, and they had the paperwork to prove it. As all of the goods were on board the ship with nothing missing from the consignment, any whisky found could not be theirs. Therefore, when found, it was looked upon as a perk of the job and swiftly removed before it was collected by the dockers.

Strangely enough, the dockers never ever complained or reported the theft of their planks. I wonder why? I have often wondered what the dockers are doing these days, now the docks and the merchant ships are gone. With their ability to hoodwink the public and appear to be doing something legitimate while actually doing something completely different, they are probably all now members of the Scottish Parliament.

Betty's Bar

B etty's Bar on Lancefield Quay, next to Queen's Dock was probably one of the best known public houses in the world in the early sixties.

Every seaman from all over the far flung corners of the world knew one sentence in English. It was, "Where is Betty's Bar please?"

This was where the ladies of the night congregated in vast numbers. In those days, they weren't all junkies, as seems to be the case nowadays, but they could all drink their share and normally did so in Betty's Bar.

There was also a spillover bar called Peter Keenan's Bar, owned by a very famous retired boxer of that name. He had won umpteen boxing titles prior to going in to the licensed trade business. His establishment was about fifty yards from Betty's Bar (it was still yards in those days, not metres). If there were several foreign ships berthed at the docks, both bars would be booming.

The foreign sailors would meet up with the working girls in the pubs and pick out the ones they fancied. They would then buy them a few drinks, agree to a price for an over-nighter, then take them back to their ship.

Most of the captains of the ships turned the proverbial Nelson blind eye to the antics of their sailors and their sleeping partners for the night. We also adopted this practice, as we had no jurisdiction aboard a foreign ship unless we were officially invited aboard by the captain. Very occasionally, and I stress extremely occasionally, when too much booze had been partaken by the sailors and the ladies of the night, and things had descended into a drunken rabble, we were invited aboard to eject the hookers.

One such rare occasion occurred on my second or third week in the police force. My eyes were quite literally opened. I was completely naive about such matters. The call came out for all night shift personnel to return to Cranstonhill Police Office to be briefed about a raid on a ship berthed in Queen's Dock. As I said earlier, this is the nearest dock to Betty's Bar.

The ship's captain had made an official request for the working girls to be removed from his ship.

"Yah beauty," said my neighbour. "You will enjoy this. It's always very funny when an official raid takes place. You will see things tonight that I can guarantee you have never seen before."

After the briefing, we made our way to the ship. We were met there by the captain who accompanied us when we boarded the vessel. This was just as well because we were as welcome as a fart in a broken down lift.

The captain led us in to the crew's quarters. I can only describe the scene as being similar to that seen in cowboy films where the saloon girls get together with the cowboys at the end of a long cattle drive. The sailors and the working girls were all drunk as skunks. The hookers were in various stages of undress, as were the sailors. The ones who were already in bed were completely naked.

The captain accompanied us as we systematically ejected the ladies, cabin by cabin. It was just as well he was with us as the crew were incandescent with rage at us spoiling their night of fun.

It appeared that most of the crew had paid the ladies up front for their services. Now here were the police throwing them off the ship before the sailors received their monies worth. (They also knew that getting a refund from the working girls was a definite no-no.)

I had rather naively presumed that, as most of the ladies were as naked as the day they were born, we would instruct them to get dressed without our presence to avoid embarrassment.

However, I was completely wrong as the older, more experienced officers simply yanked them out of the bunks, telling them to get dressed and make their way to the gangway. In fact, the only person embarrassed in the cabins was me and that didn't last very long.

The hookers were cursing and swearing at us and screaming obscenities. It appeared that every police officer on board the ship had been born out of wedlock. Fortunately for us the sailors were cursing in their native tongue which we didn't understand, although it was very obvious that they were not praising or congratulating us on our performance. In fact, but for the presence of the captain, I felt that we would all have been thrown into the murky waters of the Clyde.

Most of the ladies of the night were young and reasonably attractive, apart that is, from two ancient old crones. They had obviously both been on a lengthy dose of ugly pills which had worked perfectly. Those two old harridans were so ugly that to call them a pair of old mingers would actually have been paying them a compliment. They could only look remotely attractive to men who had been on the high seas for months with no female company, and had then drunk huge amounts of alcohol prior to meeting up with them.

Funnily enough, it was the two old wrinkled hookers who were protesting the most, principally I believe because their services were very seldom required and, unlike the younger ladies, they had not been paid in advance.

I did feel a little bit of job satisfaction, as I felt that we had at least spared two very drunk sailors from an exceedingly nasty surprise. I could only begin to imagine how they would feel when they woke up sober in the morning and found themselves lying next to those ancient, wizened, wrinkled old harlots.

Eventually, with much wailing and gnashing of teeth, we managed to evict all of the ladies from the ship. This left the captain with a very unhappy and resentful crew. However, that was his problem, as he was the one who officially requested our services.

On reflection, I could now understand my neighbour's comment when we received the call about the raid on the ship. He was absolutely right. I witnessed some of the most comical sights you could ever imagine. As I said at the beginning of this story, I quite literally had my eyes opened very wide indeed, but I would not have missed the experience for the world.

"*Doctor, I Farted Today*"

O ne of our first calls on early shift, which commenced at 6.45 a.m. and concluded at 2 p.m., was to our local family owned home bakery, run by a husband, wife and son. This of course was after we had checked out vulnerable properties and tested that the telephone and flashing blue lights were in good working order within all the police boxes (featured in Dr Who) in our beat area. These checks usually took about one hour to complete and by that time we were feeling peckish and ready for a cup of tea.

The normal procedure was that we would be ushered into the bakery area at the rear of the shop. Ron, the father would immediately instruct his wife to make a cup of tea for the boys (meaning us, of course). We would then be treated to hot rolls straight out of the oven (lovely grub), washed down by large mugs of tea.

Ron was an extremely polite, well-mannered Englishman who had resided in Scotland for over thirty years, but still retained his immaculate English accent. Ron and his son Bob were chatting away to us as usual while we were enjoying our hot rolls.

Then suddenly, Ron made his announcement. "I had to phone my doctor this morning." This received our full attention. Fearing bad news, I asked Ron why. He then told us that he had said, "Doctor, I really think you ought to know that I farted this morning."

My partner (or should I say my neighbour, as your partner was known in the early sixties) dissolved into fits of uncontrollable laughter, and I very nearly fell off my chair. The more I thought about it, the more I laughed at the pure absurdity of the whole situation; the fact that Ron had felt farting was such an important event that it was essential to phone his doctor and tell him about it.

Very soon, Ron and his son were also in hysterics when they realised just how absurd and ludicrous his statement sounded.

Eventually, I managed to compose myself enough. Trying my best to sound serious, I asked Ron if he always telephoned his doctor and told him when and where he had farted on any particular day. This if course had the effect of even more mirth from everyone. After some time, we calmed down a little and Ron explained the situation to us.

It transpired that Ron had been having trouble with his bowels; a blockage which had lasted over a week. He had in fact been due to attend hospital later that day to undergo a minor operation to unblock his passage. As it turned out, Ron had been correct to inform his doctor of his ability to fart at will that morning.

Ron's doctor was then able to cancel the operation as this was proof that the blockage was beginning to clear, and that normal service would commence quite soon with the aid of a laxative.

Poor Ron had to suffer some almighty ribbing for some time thereafter, as all of the cops asked him the same question whenever they called in for a cup of tea, namely, "Ron, did you phone your doctor today?"

Tuxedo Junction

I was out patrolling the beat one morning in Byres Road in Partick. It had been a quiet morning with no calls or incidents to attend, and the time was passing exceedingly slowly.

I was walking past the Oxfam charity shop when the manageress motioned for me to come in. She told me that she had just received a delivery that morning which might interest me.

I was intrigued to find out what the delivery was and accompanied her to the rear of the shop. She then pointed out the articles to me. Hanging up on a rail was a large number of gents evening suits, or tuxedos as they were more often called.

She advised me that she had received them from a large dress hire shop that morning and that they had been dry cleaned prior to being donated to Oxfam.

Apparently, the tuxedos were only kept for a short fixed period of time before they were replaced by brand new ones. The information that really interested me was that she intended selling them to the general public for the princely sum of £1 per tuxedo, including matching bow tie.

She told me that she didn't intend to put them on public sale until the following morning and that I was welcome to tell my friends and colleagues to call in that day if they wanted to buy an evening suit.

I used her telephone to contact my brother-in-law. He was delighted and stated that he would come over and purchase one during his lunch break.

I then looked through the tuxedos until I found one in my size. I tried it on and it fitted me perfectly, as if made to measure.

I walked over to the full-length mirror and checked myself out. There in the mirror smiling back at me was a suave, debonair James Bond type of classical well-bred gentleman. (We can all dream can't we?)

I then thanked the manageress and paid her the full purchase price of £1 (no haggling for a discount because I was her local beat man. Oh no, I insisted on paying her the full asking price). I then took my neatly parcelled evening suit back to Partick Police Office, as it was now time for my meal break.

I advised the rest of the early shift about the bargain buy during our refreshment period. I do believe that the Oxfam shop was visited by several police officers after 2 p.m. when we had completed our shift.

As it happened, purely by chance, my wife's sister, my brother-in-law, my wife and myself were attending a dinner and dance in East Kilbride's Stuart Hotel. At this time, it was a swanky, high-class establishment, unlike now where it is a pale, empty shadow of its former grandeur.

Fast forward to Saturday evening, we arrived at the hotel and were escorted to our table. My wife and sister-in-law looked gorgeous in full-length evening gowns (they were two extremely attractive young ladies).

Meanwhile, my brother-in-law and I were resplendent in our £1 tuxedos and bow ties. I thought that we looked like David Niven and Cary Grant, who were the suave sophisticated matinee idols of the sixties. They wore tuxedos with aplomb, grace and nonchalance. My wife later confessed that she thought we looked more like Laurel and Hardy.

During our very enjoyable three course dinner, I glanced surreptitiously around the room. I observed that we were the only male diners in the establishment wearing tuxedos. "Ah well," I thought to myself. "The rest of the men are not suitably dressed for a high-class dinner and dance, not like what we are" (in the words of Ernie Wise).

After the meal, the band began playing the first number of the evening and my wife suggested that we get up for the dance. As ballroom dancing was not top of my list of favourite hobbies, I normally needed several strong drinks before venturing onto the dance floor, probably because I was about as graceful and surefooted as a sumo wrestler on speed.

However, on this particular evening, I was the best dressed, most distinguished looking man in the room (apart from my brother-in-law of course). I immediately stood up and said, "Certainly, my dear. Let's show them how it is done."

This response from me took her entirely by surprise, as she usually had to ask me several times before I would even consider getting up.

Then it happened. A man beckoned me over to his table. I strolled nonchalantly over, expecting him to compliment me on my impeccable, immaculate dress sense. However, instead of complimenting me, he asked me to take a drinks order.

Totally indignant, I asked him why I should get him a round of drinks in when I was a customer just like him. "Oh, I'm sorry," he said. "I thought you were a waiter. You're dressed like one."

"I am not a waiter," I snarled back at him. "I am simply dressed in a proper and civilised manner for a dinner and dance."

"That's put him in his place," I thought to myself as we continued on towards the dance floor. However, exactly the same thing happened twice more before we even got a chance to dance.

By this time, I was hoping that the floor would open up so I could disappear through it. As I danced past the tables, I heard a fat lady remark to her company, "You don't often see a waiter up dancing when people are waiting to order a drink."

After the dance, we returned to our table where we learned that the same thing had happened to my brother-in-law.

Needless to say, neither of us sprang up for the next dance, nor the one after that. Our decision to dress in an elegant, refined manner for the dinner and dance had backfired, as we were well and truly overdressed for the low key, low budget shindig.

I only wore my £1 tuxedo one more time after that disastrous first occasion. We were hosting a family meal and social evening, and had invited my wife's cousins from Glasgow.

They duly arrived and I answered the front door, resplendent in my tuxedo and bow tie. They were of course immaculately dressed in lounge suits, shirts and ties, with the ladies in dresses.

I looked them up and down in a disdainful, critical and indignant manner and said, "I thought you knew that this was a formal black tie meal tonight."

They, of course, looked horrified and began spluttering that they hadn't been advised about this arrangement and were completely unaware that it was to be a formal meal.

They were still apologising profusely, and I was trying my best to look both annoyed and deeply upset, when my wife appeared and broke the spell. She was dressed as a bunny girl in a leotard and bunny ears.

Her attire was in no way consistent with a formal meal and they quickly realised that it had just been a wind up, after which they visibly relaxed and we all had a good laugh together.

Alas, that was the last time I wore my £1 tuxedo, as I never attended a grand enough function over the next few years where it was appropriate to wear a tuxedo and bow tie. Another reason was that I was terrified of being mistaken for a waiter again. Never mind. I still considered it to be £1 well spent.

Summer in Stranraer

I n the late seventies, it was the height of the troubles in Northern Ireland, Belfast in particular. Bombings and tit for tat attacks were an almost daily occurrence with many lives being lost on both sides of the divide.

The government at that time were apprehensive that the violence might spread over onto mainland Britain. They therefore greatly increased the police presence at the main ports for arriving and departing ferries from Northern Ireland, especially Stranraer and Port Patrick.

The procedure used was police spot checks on vehicles arriving and departing from those ports, with the main emphasis on lorries and trucks. However, the local police force could not possibly cope with the numbers of extra police personnel required to adequately police Stranraer and Port Patrick at that time.

It was therefore decided that all of the respective police forces in Scotland would supply a number of officers each month to assist the local force.

Those officers would be billeted in the luxurious, spacious five star hotel overlooking the bay in Stranraer. Not only would they reside there, but they would have full access to all the hotel facilities, including choosing all meals from the à la carte menu.

Naturally enough, the young single cops were queuing up to volunteer to spend several weeks at the seaside, living in the lap of luxury in a top of the range hotel and eating the finest food. There were also extra allowances paid for residing away from home and plenty of overtime payments thrown in. All in all, it was quite a nice little earner.

I had managed to dodge this detail for several months, primarily because I had three young daughters at primary school and my better half was not at all keen for me to disappear for several weeks, leaving her to cope with them on her own.

However, I was eventually called in and advised that I would have to take my turn, as most of my shift had been down to Stranraer several times already. I was forced to concede that they were right and that it was indeed my turn. That evening, I explained the situation to my wife and stressed how much I had tried to avoid this particular tour of duty.

Of course, she didn't believe a word of it and to be truthful, a few weeks holiday at the seaside in a luxury five star hotel did not exactly fill me with horror, although I tried manfully to pretend that it did.

In fact, the more I thought about it, the more I liked it. No one to tell me that I shouldn't eat that because it's not good for my high cholesterol count. No one to say, "Don't pour yourself another drink. You have had quite enough already." For the entire week before I left for Stranraer, I moaned how much I had tried to avoid this secondment and how extremely reluctant I was to be going there (aye, right).

For many months, I had been hearing lurid tales from the young single cops about Stranraer. According to them, the percentage of women to men was about three to one, and the young ladies were throwing themselves at them due to the shortage of local young men.

In particular, they talked about the Ugly Bug Ball in Port Patrick. This was the weekly dance night when all manner of women appeared in all sorts of shapes and sizes, looking for a lumber.

Apparently, some of the ladies were a truly awful sight to behold, and had been right at the back of the queue when beauty and good looks were being handed out.

I duly arrived in Stranraer and was briefed about our duties there by senior officers from the local force. We were then advised about the local night life in Stranraer; where to go and where not to go. There were several clubs and pubs which were well run and trouble free, but others where problems could arise and were therefore best avoided.

There were two bowling clubs, one of which was welcoming and friendly to visiting police officers, while the other one would prefer us to stay away.

I had met up with Big Jim on the bus. I had known Jim for years, although we were from different divisions within Glasgow. We were in identical situations; late thirties, married with three kids. We therefore decided to team up when off duty and stay well away from the notorious infamous man eating women of Stranraer.

That first evening, I was off duty while Big Jim was working until 8 p.m. We arranged to meet up at the friendly bowling club. I would go there at 7 p.m. and Jim would join me after he had finished his shift.

I arrived at the club and introduced myself. It was exactly as described by the local officer. They welcomed me in and absolutely insisted on giving me my first pint on the house. The club president and vice president sat down and chatted with me before inviting me to join them in a game of bowls.

It was a lovely summer's evening and we were out on the green for a couple of hours. It was standard practice for bowlers playing on the end next to the club house to keep replenishing everybody's drinks. I, of course, was an absolute stickler for the rules and made sure that our glasses were always full.

The evening wore on, but there was no sign of Big Jim showing his face, which was unusual as he was not averse to the occasional pint or two. Eventually around midnight, I thanked the club members for a thoroughly pleasant evening and wished them goodnight. They responded by inviting me back any time and to feel free to bring my colleagues with me.

I returned to the hotel and visited the resident's bar to see if Jim was still up and about. Sure enough, he was sitting there with a drink in front of him. I was about to ask him why he hadn't turned up at the bowling club when he turned the tables on me by indignantly asking me the same thing.

I couldn't believe it. He was blaming me. I retorted, "Just a cotton picking minute, sunshine. I was at the club all night. It was you who failed to appear." We then exchanged notes and it turned out that I had gone to the wrong bowling club; the one that we had been expressly warned to avoid. Big Jim, on the other hand, had spent the evening at the club recommended to us, where he had also been made very welcome.

Another evening, Jim and I visited a social club which was on the recommended list and were enjoying a quiet pint together. One of our colleagues, a young single cop, was chatting up an attractive young lady.

He came over to our table and introduced us to her, then told us that the young lady's mother and her mother's friend had bought us each a pint, wondering if we would like to join them for a drink and a chat.

We looked over and saw two very respectable looking ladies in their fifties who raised their glasses and beckoned us over. We realised that it would be rude and boorish to turn down their friendly invitation, so we walked over and joined them.

The ladies knew of course that we were visiting police officers on temporary secondment to Stranraer. We chatted amicably to them and had another couple of drinks.

Last orders had been called and we were about to wish the ladies goodnight and make our way back to the hotel. However, the waiter arrived at our table with a carry-out bag full of drink bought by the ladies. They then invited us back to their house for a nightcap before we returned to the hotel. We thanked them, but declined the offer, saying that we had an early rise in the morning.

Our young colleague then intervened, stating that he was going and surely we would not leave him on his own, talking to three ladies. Reluctantly, we agreed. As it was on our way back anyway, we would have one for the road.

We arrived at their house and sat down for the nightcap. The older ladies told us that they were both widows and had been so for many years. Our young colleague quickly finished his drink and said that he was taking the young lady for a romantic stroll along the beach.

Big Jim and I glared furiously at him. After all, we were only there at his insistence to back him up with the three ladies. He smiled cheerfully at us and swiftly left with his young companion.

During our brief conversation with our young colleague, the merry widows poured us another drink. We were not in the slightest bit worried, as the two ladies had been absolute models of decorum, respectability and good manners, with not even the tiniest hint of flirtatious behaviour or conversation.

I had almost finished my drink and was about to thank the ladies for their hospitality and head back to our hotel. However, before I got a word out, one of them beat me to the draw and quite nonchalantly stated, "Jim and I are having the upstairs bedroom and you and Betty are in the ground floor bedroom."

I froze and broke out in a cold sweat as I suddenly realised that all of the lurid tales that I had scoffed and laughed at about the sex starved ladies were actually true.

"Oh, right." I replied very nervously indeed, as I had not envisaged in my wildest imagination this particular turn of events.

I lifted my drink to my suddenly bone dry mouth and quickly considered my options. I very rapidly concluded that there was only one realistic option and that was flight.

I smiled angelically at the two ladies and said, "Excuse me, ladies. I must pay a visit to the toilet."

I stood up and made my way down the hall. The toilet was immediately adjacent to the front door. Needless to say, I walked straight past the toilet and out through the door, which I opened and shut extremely quietly.

I then took off as though the very hounds of hell were snarling and slavering at my heels. I arrived back at the hotel and went straight to the resident's bar and ordered a pint while I waited for Big Jim to join me.

It was an hour later before he arrived, glaring furiously at me and muttering obscenities which I could not possibly put down on paper.

As I had expected him back an hour ago, I asked Jim what had kept him. This of course provoked a further tirade of abuse as he described me as a treacherous, cunning sly old fox for leaving him in the lurch with the man eating merry widows.

I retorted, "If you had thought of it first, you would have been out of that front door faster than a rat up a rone pipe."

He glared at me angrily, but then started to chuckle. "Of course I would have," he chortled. "I'm only raging mad because you had the idea, you sneaky wee swine." Big Jim could be quite complimentary when he tried.

I asked him how he had managed to extricate himself from the clutches of the merry widows. He told me that he had said that I had just popped out for a breath of fresh air, and that I would return in no time, which they obviously didn't believe for a minute.

He accepted another drink while he pondered over how he could make good his escape without upsetting the ladies. He excused himself to visit the toilet, whereupon both ladies accompanied him and stood guard at the front door until he came back out.

Twenty minutes later, he had stated, "I'm sorry, ladies. This drink is going right through me. I'm afraid I'll have to visit the toilet again." Once again, they positioned themselves at the front door.

He then realised there was only one thing left to do, so he very quietly opened the toilet window, climbed out and fled the scene.

By this time, I was in uncontrollable fits of laughter, imagining Jim climbing out of the toilet window with the fearsome female double act guarding the door.

Even Jim could now see the comical side of the situation and was laughing loudly along with me. "I think," he said, "under the circumstances, the next two rounds are on you."

Needless to say, for the remainder of our stay in Stranraer, Big Jim and I gave that particular social club a very wide berth indeed. Before you ask, no, we didn't bump into the merry widows again.

Splish, Splash, We Were Taking a Bath

B ill and Bob were the regular beat men on the university beat which included Glasgow University and a large part of the surrounding area.

To describe them as large men would be a complete understatement, as they were absolutely enormous in both height and width. In parliamo Glasgow, they would be described as (and in their case, it was fully merited) being built like two brick shithouses.

The time of this event was the early sixties when policing in Glasgow was very different from what it is now. In my humble opinion, Glasgow was a much safer and happier place than it is today.

In those days, the recognised method of patrolling the beat when on the night shift, as Bill and Bob were at this time, was to thoroughly check the area for break-ins, then call in to a doss for a cup of tea. To the uninitiated, a doss was a warm, dry place where the local beat men were welcomed in with open arms and served up free food and drink.

Most of the dosses in the Marine Division were bakeries where freshly baked rolls, pies and bridies were served up with lashings of tea or coffee to wash them down. Alternatively, there were hotel kitchens and lorry driver's bed and breakfasts where sausages, bacon and eggs were on the menu. Yeah, thinking back, we sure had it tough in those days.

In the early sixties, there were no personal radios and the only way to communicate with the beat men was to flash the lights in the police boxes. The beat men then answered the police box telephone for instructions regarding them being required to attend an incident.

Therefore, not unsurprisingly, all of the best dosses were situated where the lights on the police box could be observed from a discreet distance. Bill and Bob normally had their cup of tea with Glasgow University's night watchman who had a perfect view of the police box immediately outside the main entrance.

Bill and Bob liked to relax before their tea by swimming a few lengths of the university swimming pool, while the night watchman observed the police box and immediately advised them if the lights started flashing. This enabled them to throw their uniforms on and answer the box telephone fairly quickly.

Needless to say, the beat men did not have swimming trunks. They simply stripped off to the skud and jumped in the pool as naked as the day they were born. As I said earlier, they were two enormous gargantuan men. This became even more apparent when they were skinny dipping (which I believe is the correct term for swimming in the nude). However, to describe those two huge men as skinny dippers was absolutely farcical and ludicrous in the extreme.

They resembled two elephant seals in size and shape and swam with all the grace of two drunken hippos. On this particular morning, the regular cleaning lady, who was well used to seeing the two enormous figures splashing up and down the pool, was off sick and there was a young, attractive lady standing in for her.

The night watchman had forgotten to tell the young lady about Bill and Bob, although I am fairly sure that he wanted to see what her reaction would be when she saw them in all their naked glory.

She strolled in and walked along the side of the pool. Suddenly catching sight of the naked swimmers, she screamed hysterically and leapt in the air shouting, "Help, police, help, police, please help me!"

The terrified young cleaner had picked an unfortunate time to arrive at the pool, as the hairy swimmers had just completed a length swimming breast stroke. That would have been terrifying enough with their huge buttocks in view, but they had now begun a length of backstroke with their large dangly bits splishing and a splashing on full display.

It was at that point that Bill uttered the immortal phrase, "Don't worry madam. There is nothing to be frightened about. We are your local beat men." By this time the night watchman had arrived. He calmed her down by telling her that they were police officers, and that they did this almost every morning.

Bill and Bob were suitably mortified and embarrassed by the very obvious fright suffered by the young cleaner, especially as the regular cleaner simply got on with her job without giving them a second glance. They clambered out of the pool and got dressed as quickly as possible.

They rather sheepishly approached the watchman's office, unsure of what sort of a reception they would receive from the young lady after her screams of terror at the sight of them. Fortunately, the young lady had by now seen the funny side of the situation and had been laughing uproariously about it while they were getting dressed.

However, when Bill and Bob walked in, she decided to get her own back on them. With as straight a face as possible, she said, "Oh, thank goodness. It's the police at last. I want to report a case of indecent exposure by two naked men."

Unfortunately for her, she was unable to keep a straight face and began to grin broadly.

Bill cottoned on right away and in his most solemn official police officer voice replied, "How terribly upsetting for you madam. Can you describe these two men?" "Yes, of course I can," replied the young lady. "They were two hulking enormous brutes and I was absolutely terrified out of my wits. In fact, come to think of it, they were about the same height and build as yourselves."

"Thank you madam," said Bill. "You don't get too many of our size to the pound. Do you think you could pick them out at an identification parade?" "Most certainly," she replied. "But they would have to be dressed exactly as they were."

Bill said, "We will definitely arrange that if we find them, although I am fairly sure that they will have made good their escape by now."

"Yes I agree," she responded. "I'm sure there is absolutely no chance of you finding them now. Why don't you just sit down and have a cup of tea with us?" "Thank you madam," said Bill as they all sat down smiling broadly at each other. "We don't mind if we do."

Chust A Ceevy

This story is about Big Duncan, who like many City of Glasgow police officers in the 1960s, came from one of the islands of the western Isles. He was a real highland gentleman who would never dream of insulting anyone by refusing the offer of food or drink.

On the day in question, Duncan was on Sunday morning early shift, the quietest, most boring time of the week. In the sixties, the typical Glaswegian enjoyed a good bevvy on a Saturday night and slept late on a Sunday morning. As per usual, there had been no calls or incidents of any kind during Duncan's monotonous morning and he was looking forward to going off duty at 2 p.m.

He was visited by the section sergeant and received a signature in his notebook to signify that he was diligently carrying out his beat duties.

As it was raining heavily and the streets were deserted, Duncan then decided to take a stroll past an ex serviceman's club on his beat and see if there were any signs of life there.

As luck would have it, inside the club at that time were three of his friends. They spotted Big Duncan strolling past and knocked on the window, beckoning him to come in. Duncan of course knew the manager and staff of the club very well, as he had to call at the club occasionally to, "Ahem," enquire if everything was in order.

The usual procedure was to invite the beat man in for a chat to discuss any problems within the club, and of course as a matter of courtesy, offer a refreshment which was almost always accepted.

The manager ushered Duncan into his private office and asked him if he could manage a wee drop of the Cratur. Big Duncan of course politely accepted, as a refusal could possibly offend and he simply hated to upset anyone.

A short time later, Duncan looked at his watch and realised it was almost time to report to the police box and ring himself off duty. He left the manager's office and spoke to his friends who of course invited him to join them for a social drink.

Big Duncan demurred, explaining that he was not yet off duty. They of course insisted that he returned to the club after his shift. The manager agreed with them, telling Duncan that he could deposit his hat and tunic in his office. He would then lend him a jacket to allow him to join his friends out of uniform. This suggestion appealed to Big Duncan greatly. It was just what the doctor ordered; the perfect way to finish off his shift.

Off he went to the police box which was situated right on the Y junction where Sauchiehall Street meets Argyle Street.

Duncan cheerfully entered the police box and sat down on the stool. He had a short while to wait before he could lift the internal telephone and ring himself off duty. He looked at his watch and smiled; only one minute to go. However, unknown to him, things were just about to get exceedingly difficult.

Immediately outside the police box, the traffic lights malfunctioned and switched off. Blissfully unaware, Duncan phoned himself off duty at exactly 2 p.m.

Whistling cheerfully and looking forward to discarding his uniform and joining his friends for a convivial afternoon in the club, he opened the police box door and stepped out.

Absolute bedlam ensued right before his incredulous eyes. Cars travelling westwards on Sauchiehall Street and Argyle Street both presumed that they had the right of way. The leading cars from each street collided with each other, while three cars closely following were unable to stop and slammed into them.

Big Duncan was horrified, visualising himself writing up a road traffic report about the accident. He swiftly worked out that the incident involved eight vehicles, eight drivers, sixteen passengers and various eye witnesses around the junction. It would take several hours of work to write up the report. This would certainly cancel out his afternoon in the club with his friends.

By now, he was surrounded by all the people involved. Thinking very quickly, he advised them that it was unfortunate, but he had just gone officially off duty, and that under road traffic regulations, he was not permitted to deal with this incident (tut, tut, naughty, naughty).

He then told them not to worry as he would contact Partick Police Office and have an on duty police officer attend immediately. Luckily for Duncan, they were completely taken in by his inventive explanation. In fact, most of them were saying how helpful the nice policeman was, and him officially off duty too.

Duncan then returned to the police box, but didn't enter it. The telephone inside the box was on an internal line, used only by police officers. Duncan did not want to use it because he knew, as he was at the scene when it occurred, he would be instructed to deal with the accident.

In those days, (and still now) all members of the public, regardless of their professions or occupations, were referred to as civilians or civvies if they were not serving police officers.

Duncan therefore went to the flap on the outside which contained a telephone for use by the public to contact the police. He lifted the telephone and, speaking in the most polite voice he could muster, spoke to the police telephonist.

He told her that he would like to report an accident involving a number of vehicles and could they please send out a police officer to deal with it immediately. Naturally enough, the telephonist recognised Big Duncan's voice, despite his best efforts to disguise it.

She asked him mischievously, "Could you give me your name and address please caller?" Quick as a flash, Duncan replied, "I'm chust a ceevy reporting an accident."

He swiftly replaced the telephone before the telephonist could reply. Duncan then advised the waiting crowd that a police officer would attend immediately.

He then hurriedly left the scene and returned to the club. His friends asked him if everything went smoothly. "Och aye," replied Duncan. "I chust walked to the box and phoned myself off duty, then I came straight back again, and make mine a large one please."

I Think I Am Snookered

It was another Sunday morning early shift; cold, bleak and wet. The streets in Partick were absolutely empty apart from an occasional vehicle passing through Byres Road. There were no pedestrians to be seen apart from the two soaking wet beat men who were trudging up the road.

Mr Magoo and his neighbour Andy decided to get out of the rain for a while and made their way to the snooker hall in Great George Street, just off Byres Road. There was a night watchman on duty inside the premises who remained there until the hall opened up for business in the afternoon.

The watchman was delighted to see the beat men, as it broke up the tedious boredom of his very long and lonely shift. The normal procedure was that the beat men played a frame along with their cup of tea and chat, so he immediately put on the kettle and switched the lights on above the snooker table next to his office.

Andy was an exceedingly slim young man. In fact, to be brutally honest, he was so skinny that he could easily have featured as the eight stone weakling who regularly got sand kicked in his face by the beach bully.

Andy was so thin that he couldn't wear just a belt to keep his trousers up. He also needed a pair of braces under his uniform. It was rather unkindly rumoured that

Andy had worn a pair of deep sea diver's boots when he was weighed for his entrance physical examination, prior to joining the police force.

Anyway, to get back to the story, the beat men took off their raincoats and tunics to have a game of snooker. Andy also slipped his braces off his shoulders, as they restricted his snooker action.

The frame of snooker had only been in progress for a few minutes when Andy received a call on his personal radio. It was from the section sergeant asking for Andy's position so that he could sign his notebook.

Bold and shrewd, Andy stated that he was checking property in the lane behind Great George Street. The sergeant replied, "Roger, attending from close to that locus." Locus is the police speak for location.

Andy almost choked on his tea. He frantically pulled on his tunic and hat, then ran for the back door which opened onto the lane. He was desperate to get into the lane before the sergeant arrived and spotted him coming out of the snooker hall.

Andy managed to reach the rear of one of the shops and was diligently checking the padlocks just as the sergeant arrived in the lane in his panda car.

Andy turned to face the sergeant with a triumphant smirk on his face, knowing that for once he had managed to pull a fast one on his superior officer.

The sergeant stepped out of the car and gave Andy a very quizzical look. He then stated, "I hope I haven't called you at an inconvenient time when you were just in the middle of a game of snooker."

Andy thought frantically, then decided that there was no way that the sergeant could have known that he was playing snooker. He therefore tried his best to look deeply hurt by the the flippant remark and replied, "Of course not sergeant. I am simply checking out the property on my beat in a proper and diligent manner."

"Aye, right," said the sergeant sarcastically. "You're checking out property in the rain without a raincoat and getting yourself soaked."

Andy had not had time to put his raincoat back on.

The sergeant added, "Ask your neighbour why I knew you were playing snooker." He then signed Andy's notebook, jumped back into the panda car and drove off.

Thoroughly chastened, bewildered and bemused, Andy wondered why the sergeant had immediately accused him of playing snooker. After all, when he had arrived in the lane, Andy had been checking property.

Andy made his way back to the snooker hall and found his neighbour and the night watchman in fits of uncontrollable, hysterical laughter.

Andy couldn't understand what was so funny until they pointed to his knees. He looked down and cringed with embarrassment. In fact, he was well and truly mortified. Hanging down, several inches below his knees, were his braces.

"Oh no," exclaimed Andy to Mr Magoo who was still in fits of laughter. "Why didn't you tell me before I went out to see the sergeant?"

Mr Magoo replied, "Because it wouldn't have nearly been so funny if I had told you."

Mr Magoo, I should add, had a wicked sense of humour.

Bus Stop

I had only recently transferred to the Strathclyde Police Courts Branch, Glasgow Area. At that time, they were based within the original Glasgow Sheriff Court Building situated in Ingram Street, right in the middle of Glasgow city centre.

I was nearing the end of my probationary period. Imagine, here I was, a veteran police officer with over twenty years police service back on probation again.

The reason for this was because it was a much sought after position with a large number of police officers on the waiting list.

The perks were patently obvious. No more late, early or night shifts, and being on duty three out of four weekends every month. Instead, we worked day shift hours Monday to Friday and were off duty every Saturday and Sunday. To put more icing on the cake, we would be asked to perform overtime on Saturday afternoons at either Ibrox or Parkhead, depending on which member of the Old Firm were playing a home game.

As Saturday was our official day off, we were paid an enhanced weekly rest day rate and were still off duty every Saturday night. I could therefore make arrangements to go out socially for the first time in over twenty years.

Naturally enough, I was very anxious to serve out my probation period smoothly and be inducted as a full time court staff officer at the end of it.

The one totally unbreakable rule which resulted in an officer being returned to their division was a simple one. Under no circumstances could they allow an accused person in their custody to escape from court. I was extremely aware of this rule and guarded all prisoners in my custody with my full attention.

The policing arrangements at the Old Glasgow Sheriff Court building were as follows:

A court staff officer was detailed to run a particular court in the building, assisted by either one or two "Redskins".

Redskins were the affectionate titles given to the police officers who were temporarily seconded from their divisions to assist regular court staff officers on a weekly basis. I believe this was because the full time court staff were looked upon as the chiefs and the divisional officers as the indians.

The redskins normally came in two categories. (1) An officer very close to the end of their thirty years police service and looking forward to retirement or (2) An officer on light duties due to ill health or long term injury and not fit for normal duties on the beat.

On this particular day, I had just two accused persons appearing in my court on prison warrants. A prison warrant meant that both the accused were at present serving a custodial sentence and had to return to prison, irrespective of the outcome of their court appearance.

I therefore had only one redskin assisting me that day instead of the normal two officers. Unfortunately for me that morning, I had an officer who was a lovely man, but fitted both categories, i.e. only two months left before his retirement and on light duties after being involved in a road traffic accident.

That meant that he had a severe limp and an extremely slow and laborious walking action. In the unlikely event of a race between a tortoise and my redskin, I would have bet my house on the tortoise.

On that particular morning, I was also in trouble, suffering from a chronic and painful attack of gout in the big toes of both of my feet.

Everyone thinks that gout is a very comical ailment. That is, unless you happen to suffer from it. I can only describe the pain as being similar to severe toothache, only magnified twenty times over.

This was the final week of my probation before becoming a permanent member of the court staff. Therefore, I didn't want to rock the boat by going off sick with only two days to go.

Consequently, we were both treading very gingerly whilst going about our court duties. Still, we were managing to cope until, that is, the two prison warrants appeared before the sheriff.

The accused were young men aged about twenty years of age and fit as fiddles. They were appearing at court to be sentenced on different crimes for which they were already serving a period of imprisonment. They were feeling very confident, even cocky. Their lawyer had told them that the sheriff would almost certainly impose a concurrent sentence. This would then allow them both to be released before Christmas.

A concurrent sentence runs in tandem along with any other sentence which an accused may be serving. It is very similar to the supermarket offer of buy one get one free.

Unfortunately for them, the sheriff didn't agree with the lawyer and imposed an additional consecutive sentence. A consecutive sentence does not begin until any other prison sentence has been completed.

This meant that they would certainly spend Christmas plus several months more inside "The Big House" as Barlinnie Prison was known.

We then handcuffed the two accused together to escort them back to the cells. They were not happy bunnies. In fact, they were almost apoplectic with rage, cursing and swearing at their defence solicitor and blaming him for their additional period of imprisonment.

They appeared to have forgotten the old saying:

If you can't do the time, don't do the crime.

There were no secure passage areas direct from the court to the cells area, as there are within the new Glasgow Sheriff Court. Instead, we had to escort prisoners through public areas for a considerable distance before reaching the cells.

We were just passing the top of the main stairway leading to the front doors when it happened. I was hailed by the sheriff's clerk from our court. He approached me with the official prison warrant which sealed the two prisoners' fate for a further stay in Barlinnie Prison.

I half turned to accept the warrant, whereupon all hell broke loose. The two prisoners wrenched themselves from our grip and ran towards the main staircase. They were handcuffed together and were very obviously in custody. I therefore rather naively assumed that members of the public would assist us to apprehend the two men and prevent them from escaping.

I shouted out, "Stop those men. They are in official police custody." Unfortunately for me, my confidence in the public was sadly misplaced. Instead of assisting me, they simply stood aside and opened up like the Red Sea, forming a clear pathway for the fleeing prisoners.

The looks I received from the public were very clear. I could almost hear them saying, "Aye, that will be right. No chance."

My redskin and I pursued the men down the stairway and out through the main entrance doors onto Ingram Street. My redskin's limp became far more pronounced when he tried to break in to an exceedingly slow and laborious jog.

I sprinted past him. Sprinted, that's a laugh. Remember, I was suffering from severe gout in both feet. My running action was like a cat on a hot tin roof. Every stride I took was agony.

However, despite my intense pain, I was determined to catch them. I knew that if they managed to escape from my custody, I would be transferred straight back to my division.

The two prisoners were now feeling quite cocky. They had obviously spotted that we were not members of the Olympic sprint relay squad. They looked round and one of them shouted "Haw, funny polis. Limpy and Gimpy. Get it right up you."

Fortunately for me and my future career, their cockiness proved to be their undoing. They turned back round and saw a bus stop pole right in front of them. They ran past the pole on either side of it, forgetting that they were handcuffed together.

This brought them to a shuddering halt as they swung round the pole and crashed into each other, banging their heads together before sliding down the bus stop and falling on to the pavement in a quivering, twitching heap.

This allowed me to hop, skip and jump over to them. I smiled sweetly and said, "Nice of you to stop, boys. Are you waiting for a bus?"

I grabbed the men with a vice-like grip that a team of cart horses could not shift. I was then joined by my old redskin who limped up, peching and panting like a steam engine.

We then frogmarched the now thoroughly chastened prisoners straight back to the cells.

I was absolutely delighted to clang the cell door closed on them, saying, "We are not quite such funny polis now, are we lads?"

Two days later, I received my permanent transfer to the court staff, although I never did find out whether I was Limpy or Gimpy.

Sausage Sannies

This particular case only came to the sheriff and jury court because of the severity of the injury sustained by the injured party, namely a life threatening fractured skull.

The accused in the case was a middle-aged lady of impeccable character. Until now, she had led a completely blameless life and had never been in trouble of any kind.

The evidence led by the procurator fiscal was that the injured party in the trial was the brother of the now accused woman.

He had been residing with his sister and brother-in-law on a temporary basis, having been thrown out of his own house by his wife. On the day of the serious assault, there had been an altercation between the brother and sister. This had resulted in her striking him on the head with an object and thereby fracturing his skull.

The accused in the case elected to give evidence in her own defence and took the stand. Her evidence was as follows:

"Ah took my brother in, so ah did, to gie him a chance tae make it up wie his wife. Ah wasnae in the least bit surprised when she threw him oot because he's a lazy wee drunkard, so he is, and ahm only surprised that it took her that long tae dae it."

"Please carry on," said her defence lawyer.

"He had been staying wie me for about three weeks and had never even once put his haun in his pocket tae pay anything towards his keep, and he eats like a horse, so he does. On the day of our argument, I told him that if he didnae put his haun in his pocket and bring in some messages, (for English readers, messages are groceries) he was getting the bums rush from oor hoose tae."

"He came back in tae the hoose at lunchtime when I was in the middle of cooking sausages for my husband who, unlike my brither, works every hour that God sends."

"He wis carrying a plastic bag and I said tae him I hope that's messages for the hoose in that bag. He said, 'Aye it is. It's a hauf bottle and six cans of lager, so it is.' He then said, 'Sausage sannies, munchy, munchy. Jeest what ah wis feeling like.'"

At this point her defence lawyer interjected and asked her, "And what was your reply to your brother?"

"Ah said there will be nae munchy munchy for you, you lazy drunken wee get. These sausages are for my man. He's been oot working since six o'clock this morning, so he has."

Her lawyer prompted her again, saying, "In your own words, tell the court what happened next."

She replied, "Well, you would hardly believe it, so you wouldnae, but the cheeky, lazy, drunken wee get lifted a sausage sannie aff my man's plate and took a big bite oh it, so he did."

"Yes, carry on," said her lawyer.

She continued, "Well, I was that angry, so ah wis, that I hit him on his head. It was just pure bad luck that I happened to be holding the frying pan wie the sausages in it at the time."

Her defence agent then stated, "Then I take it that at no time did you intend to inflict a serious injury to your brother during this unfortunate incident."

"Of course not," retorted the accused. "He's a lazy drunken wee bampot, but he is still my brother, so he is."

I was finding it very difficult, in fact nearly impossible, to keep a straight face. I looked around the courtroom and could see that everyone was having similar difficulties, including the presiding sheriff.

The prosecution and the defence addressed the jury on the respective merits of the case before them. The sheriff then briefly addressed the jury. He made it very clear that the accused had admitted the assault, but advised them that they could return a guilty verdict under provocation if they were so inclined.

The jury were out for a very short time and when they returned, they predictably found the accused guilty under intense, severe provocation.

The defence lawyer then stood up and made a plea in mitigation due to the severe provocation on the part of the injured party towards the accused.

The brother of the accused stood up from the public benches and addressed the sheriff. He said, "Yer Honour, could I say something before you pass sentence?"

The sheriff replied, "Because of the unusual circumstances of this case, and that the accused and yourself are siblings, I will allow you to make a very brief statement. Please go ahead."

The brother stated, "Every word that my sister has said is the gospel truth. My brother-in-law and her don't even drink and the only thing I ever brought back tae their hoose wis a carryoot. Ah did say munchy, munchy and I did hae a big bite oh his sausage sanny. I don't think she even realised that she still had the frying pan in her haun when she swung it at me, so she never."

The man continued, "That's all I have to say, yer Honour. I wis definitely due a slap for what I done, although maybe a fractured skull wis a bit over the top."

He then sat down and the defence lawyer stood up and said, "I do believe that the injured party has indeed admitted severe and gross provocation. I will now leave the matter of sentence in this case to your Lordship."

The sheriff then stated, "You have been found guilty of an assault that resulted in severe injury to the victim. However, in this case, I find that the degree of provocation suffered by you was indeed intense, and I can well understand why your nerve snapped momentarily. Also, I am convinced that you will never appear before this court again. Therefore, I will not impose any further punishment upon you. I will now simply admonish you. You are now free to leave the courtroom."

The lady thanked the sheriff for his understanding of the situation and stepped out of the dock. She then walked over to her brother, linked arms with him and they walked out of the courtroom, smiling at each other as they went.

Silence in Court

I t was the end of a very long and protracted sheriff and jury trial at Glasgow Sheriff Court. It had appeared likely for a large part of the trial that the career criminal who was the accused was going to get away with yet another number of violent and nasty crimes against society.

Eye witnesses to the crimes were terrified to identify the accused because of his very well-earned reputation for violence. Most of the witnesses in the case gave evidence in a comparable style. They all stated that he looked similar to the man they had observed committing the crimes, but they could not swear on oath that it was definitely the accused sitting in the dock.

This was absolutely perfect for the defence Queen's Counsel who would then stand up and make their closing speech to the jury in the following fashion:

"Ladies and gentlemen of the jury. Thank you for the close attention that you have given to the evidence in this case. I am entirely certain that it cannot have escaped your attention that eye witness identification has been very poor throughout this trial. None of the main prosecution witnesses has been absolutely certain that the gentleman (aye, right. Pull the other one, why don't you?) sitting in the dock was definitely the man they saw committing the crimes libelled against him."

"Therefore, how can you be certain beyond any possible question of doubt that my client was indeed that man? Remember, if there is the slightest, even the most infinitesimal shred of a doubt, then you cannot find him guilty."

Fortunately, for the sake of justice, the police forensic evidence was very strong and compelling, despite the weak evidence from the very frightened eye witnesses. This evidence placed him fairly and squarely at the scene of every crime, and the jury was well aware of that. They were then addressed by the sheriff and instructed to retire to the jury room to consider their verdict.

The sheriff in this trial liked to call a spade a spade. He always insisted on witnesses using the exact words that were used at a crime scene and simply would not tolerate euphemisms in their place.

Therefore, if a witness said that the accused said, "Effing this," or, "Eff you, pal," he or she was quickly stopped by the sheriff. He insisted on the actual swear words being used to duplicate exactly the phrases used at the crime scene by the accused, and could not make true decision unless he heard an exact verbatim account.

The jury returned to the court with a guilty verdict on all of the crimes libelled against him, much to the surprise and consternation of the accused. He had believed that the jury would be too frightened to bring in a guilty verdict.

The sheriff clerk then read out all of the previous convictions of the accused, which were considerable and drew gasps of astonishment from the jury.

I now apologise for the following expletives, but they are entirely necessary to fully describe the comical misunderstanding that ensued within the court.

The sheriff instructed the accused to stand up and warned him that, with his long and extensive record of crime, he was considering a lengthy period of imprisonment. He then asked him, "Have you anything you wish to say before I pass sentence."

The accused snarled back at the sheriff, "Fuck all!"

The sheriff then addressed the police officer who was standing in the dock beside the accused. "What did the accused say Officer?"

The police officer replied, "The accused said fuck all M'Lord."

The sheriff mused reflectively and replied, "Thank you, Officer, but I was sure that I heard him say something."

The police officer realised that the sheriff had misunderstood and tried to assist him by again saying, "The accused said fuck all, M'Lord."

"Yes, yes, I know he didn't say anything," said the sheriff irritably. "You have already told me that."

He then sentenced the accused to a lengthy period of imprisonment and the police officer swiftly removed him from the court before he could say another word.

The Bachelors' Party

O n this particular occasion, I was on night duty with my neighbour Jimmy who later went on to become Scottish Indoor Bowling Champion, winning several international titles. We had dealt with the drunken fights and squabbles that always occurred on Friday and Saturday nights in Glasgow.

The licensing laws were very different in the sixties, as all the pubs were forced to close at 10 p.m. This meant that there was frantic activity just before closing time with treble rounds of drinks being ordered up by all of the punters. In those days, they were allowed ten minutes drinking up time before they were swiftly ushered out of the licensed premises onto the streets, which meant they had to swallow it all before ten past ten.

This system of course resulted in huge hordes of people all leaving the pubs at exactly the same time. Naturally enough, having consumed treble or quadruple rounds of booze in the ten minutes before leaving, the drink quickly took effect when they hit the fresh air. People who had been sitting inside those licensed establishments having deeply meaningful intellectual conversations turned into gibbering drunks outside.

However, in those days in Glasgow, the vast majority of the pub-goers were a good natured crowd and there wasn't too much serious trouble. In most cases, a word in their ear was enough to sort out the squabbles and point them in the direction of home.

On this particular evening, we had been assisted by the policeman's best friend, heavy rain, which dispersed the crowds much quicker than dozens of cops.

It was now the early hours of the morning and apart from a couple of amorous cats yewling up a lane, (the cats were yewling, not us) the streets were completely empty.

The rain was still pounding down, so we decided it was time for a seat and a cup of tea. We popped in to the Lorne Hotel in Sauchiehall Street, close to its junction with Argyle Street, as we knew that Andy, the night manager, would still be up and about.

We entered the hotel to find a show business party in full swing. In those far off days, television was still in its infancy and the Glasgow theatres were booming, attracting full houses every night.

Andy ushered us to the manager's office, or rather he tried to, as our path was blocked by all kinds of celebrities who were in a jovial, convivial mood and enjoying the party.

After chatting to many of them, we were introduced to the "Top Of The Bill" act in Glasgow at that time, The Bachelors. They were one of the original boy bands. The group consisted of three handsome young men from Ireland. The group consisted of 2 brothers called Con and Dec Clusky and their close friend John Stokes.

In the late sixties, The Bachelors were every bit as popular and famous as Westlife is today. Yes, time moves on, but some things remain the same.

We had been chatting to them for some time when the news filtered through that the alcohol was finished and more was required to keep the party going. As the party was at their behest, The Bachelors decided that it was up to them to obtain more strong drink. Their latest single was at number one and they were appearing on Top of the Pops that week.

Con and Dec both had a large glass of whisky in their hands and were frightened to put them down, now that the party had run out of alcohol.

Con handed me his drink for safekeeping while Dec handed my neighbour Jimmy his. Con then leaned over to me and stated in an exaggerated stage whisper (I told you it was a show business party) "You John, are the only one in here that I would trust to look after my drink." I assured him that I would guard it with my life and have it waiting for him when he returned.

The reason they had to leave the Lorne Hotel to obtain more drink was because the day shift Hotel Manager always locked up the bar before leaving and Andy did not have a key (probably a very wise decision on his part).

Some time had passed and The Bachelors had not returned. Con's glass was now becoming very heavy in my hand. However, I had no sooner polished off Con's very large whiskey when the bachelors returned empty-handed. The first thing Con said was, "We couldn't buy any alcohol anywhere. Thank goodness we left our whiskey in your safe keeping as we are desperate for a drink."

His face fell when I held up his empty glass and Jimmy held up Dec's, also of course completely empty.

"You dirty rotten scoundrels," said Con. (That was the gist of his statement but I do believe there were a great number of expletives as well!) "To think we trusted you."

"Never mind Con," I replied. "You have learned a very valuable lesson tonight." "Oh, yes, and what might that be?" he asked sarcastically. "You have learned that when it comes to strong drink, you can't trust anyone," said I.

Con thought about it for a moment, then he began to chuckle. "You're right John, you're right. You do learn something new every day."

A few days later, I watched The Bachelors performing their number one song on Top of the Pops and wondered if they had learned anything new today.

Perfect For Parsnips

T his particular tale happened in the early sixties. It was a Saturday. There was an international football match taking place that day at Hampden between Scotland and England, and I was on duty at it.

It had been taken for granted by the massive Scottish support at the match that their team would beat England. In those far off days, Scotland was not regarded as the underdog as it most certainly is now.

In the sixties, Scotland was endowed with dozens of world class football players who would get a game with any team in the world. All of the successful teams in England were packed with Scottish players, unlike now where they are as rare as hen's teeth. It therefore came as no surprise that they comprehensively gubbed the "Auld Enemy" that day.

Although there was a huge turnout of police personnel, the game was always played in the best of spirits, as this was a time before the football hooligans had begun to plague football, and eventually cause this particular fixture between the two countries to be abandoned.

Every police division normally supplied a full shift of officers, as in those far off halcyon days, it was always a full house at Hampden. This was long before all-seated football stadiums, and it was quite common to have crowds of over one hundred and fifty thousand attending, particularly when we were playing England.

The procedure was that the entire early shift finished early and made their way over to Hampden, while the back shift officers started early to cover for them. Each division had specific duties and areas of Hampden to police.

The entire Mounted Police Division always attended at those fixtures, and were an absolute Godsend to ourselves who were on foot patrol. Quite often, as we attempted to keep the queues of supporters waiting at the turnstiles apart, there were surges of huge numbers of punters and we were in severe danger of being crushed. That was the cue for the horses to move in. They walked through the masses like a hot knife through butter. The ones who saw the horses approaching frantically tried to scramble out of their way, while the others were unceremoniously swatted aside like an annoying swarm of flies. They were able to clear a space around a crushed cop in literally seconds and we were delighted to see them.

The game itself had gone smoothly with practically no trouble whatsoever from the massive crowd. This meant that we were able to observe the game along with the amicable, good natured supporters. Scotland was well on top and winning comfortably. All in all, it had been an almost perfect afternoon. Four hours overtime, absolutely no crowd trouble, able to watch the match in peace and quiet, and watch Scotland pulverise England. What was not to like about it?

At the conclusion of the match, we saw the supporters in our area safely and quietly out of the stadium. Our division was then stood to attention, checked that all of our personnel were present and correct, then dismissed from duty.

It was then up to us to make our own way home by underground, car, bus or by police vehicle back to our police office and leave from there. Personally, I was planning to make my way home by bus. However, this was virtually impossible, as there were literally hundreds of supporters waiting at every bus stop.

However, I had one thing in my favour. I was an officer of the law in full police uniform. This I used to my full advantage. The traffic was slow moving and stopping frequently at traffic lights. I therefore walked up to a bus which had stopped for a few seconds and motioned to the driver to open the doors and let me in. He beckoned me in with the usual parliamo Glasgow greeting, "In you come, big yin." This wasn't easy as the bottom deck of the bus boasted much more than its permitted capacity, with passengers squashed up against each other like sardines.

The driver winked at me and said, "Don't worry Officer. There is plenty room for you upstairs." I replied, "Good on you. That will do me nicely," and forced my way through the heaving masses. I climbed the stairs and peered into the upper deck. To my complete and utter surprise, I observed Big Bill, my shift colleague from our division, sitting in splendid isolation about half way along the bus. He spotted me and called out, "Ah, it's John the Hat. Come and join me brother."

I should add that Big Bill had a poor memory for names and was in the habit of calling his colleagues either "brother" or "young fella" when he spoke to them. I took another step up the stairs and then it hit me. It was like putting my head into a solid wall of smell. It was overpowering in its intensity and stank to the high heavens of fresh reeking shit.

Big Bill spotted me recoiling in horror and motioned me to approach him. I slowly and gingerly walked towards him and noticed that he appeared to be steaming. I don't mean as in the Glasgow meaning of steaming, i.e. being very inebriated, rather that he quite literally had little puffs of steam floating up on either side of him and a small cloud of steam forming above his head.

I now fully appreciated why there were no passengers on the upper deck apart from Big Bill and was desperately trying to work out how I could get back down the stairs without hurting his feelings. He leaned over and patted the seat on the other side of the passage saying, "Sit here brother. I don't want you sitting beside me and squashing my fertiliser."

At last, I could now see what was causing the overpowering, nauseating stench. There had been some rain that day and we were wearing our police raincoats. Now, police raincoats have enormous, voluminous pockets for carrying all manner of things. Today, Big Bill's pockets were brimming over with fresh, hot, steaming horse droppings.

"This is just some fertiliser for my vegetables," said Bill. "My parsnips and rhubarb love it." "That's not fertiliser," I retorted. "It's dung. In fact, it's not just dung, it's hot, steaming fresh shit. And anyway, I prefer custard with my rhubarb." "Yes, yes, I know," said Bill. "But it's absolutely perfect for my parsnips."

As the smell was so strong, you could almost chew it, I kept my mouth shut until the double decker bus pulled into the next stop. I then excused myself by lying with a straight face that I had to change to another bus to make my way home. I jumped off the bus and waited for the next one; the same number bus going to the same destination. The second bus smelled strongly of sweat, beer and cigarettes, but in comparison, it was as fresh as a daisy.

EPILOGUE:

A couple of months later, Big Bill brought in a basket of parsnips and placed them on the table, telling everyone in our shift to help themselves, as he had a bumper crop and couldn't use them all himself. To be fair to him, the parsnips looked wonderful shiny, practically bursting out of their skins.

However, I knew what the little blighters had been feeding on for the last two months and very politely allowed the other members of our shift to claim them. I couldn't stop thinking of the old saying, "As happy as a pig in shit," and changing it to, "As happy as a parsnip in shit."

The following day, there were rave reviews of Bill's parsnips from the shift. He sought me out and asked me if I had enjoyed them and for the second time with an absolutely straight poker face, I told him a bare-faced lie. "They were scrumptious Bill." "Good on you brother," he replied. "I'll bring you in some rhubarb when it's ready." "Oh, thanks very much Bill," I said, trying my utmost to keep a solemn face. "I will really look forward to that."

Down in the Crypt

I was on night shift from Sunday evening until Monday morning. As it was about 1 a.m. and pouring down with rain, the streets were now completely empty.

Partick at this time was a working class area of Glasgow in the very best meaning of the title. The vast majority of the inhabitants worked and unemployment levels were practically zero. Therefore, these good citizens were nearly all tucked up in bed in preparation for the start of another week's work.

The torrential rain was also assisting us, as the housebreakers preferred to carry out their nefarious activities in dry weather. As we were now dripping wet, we decided it was time to get in out of the rain for a while.

As luck would have it, there was an all-night cinema on our beat, so we decided to call in and check that the licensing regulations were being adhered to. We were very zealous about checking out licensed premises during outbreaks of heavy rain.

We made our way upstairs to the balcony which was closed to customers during the night. Alan, my neighbour was listening to the recently issued police personal radio with the sound turned down low, in case we received a call to attend an incident.

The film in progress was one of the Dracula horror films which were very popular at that time. The scene was set deep down in the basement of an old gothic style mansion. The hero of the film, probably Van Helsing, was armed with a wooden stake and a hammer. He was seeking out the lair of Dracula, hoping to find and dispose of him before nightfall. Unfortunately for him, the shadows were falling outside the creepy old house and the sun was dipping down below the horizon. It was just about to change from dusk to nightfall.

The scene then changed to show Dracula's coffin sitting on soil from Transylvania as it grew darker and darker.

I glanced over at Alan and saw that he was holding the personal radio close to his ear, listening to it intently. He suddenly leapt to his feet and ran towards the stairs. I immediately bounded after him with the speed and grace of a gazelle (I sometimes exaggerate just a little).

We then ran down the stairs like two Olympic sprinters. The manager and the usherette were standing in the foyer as we thundered towards them. They jumped out of our way as we swept past them like greyhounds chasing a rabbit.

We ran down the outside cinema stairs and into the street where I managed to catch up with Alan and grab him by his arm. I asked him if we had received an emergency call on the radio and if so, what was the nature of the emergency? He looked a little shamefaced before replying, "No, we haven't received a call." I was now completely baffled and asked, "Then why are we running about like escaped lunatics in the pouring rain?"

Alan replied, "I just had to get out of there quickly before it happened." I was now thoroughly confused. "Before what happened?" "Well," he replied. "I just knew the coffin lid was going to creak open and Dracula would sit up, and that absolutely terrifies me." He went on to explain that he would have had nightmares for months if he had actually seen Dracula within his coffin.

"That's a pity," I said. "Because that's the only place on our beat that is open at this time in the morning. We can't go back in after we nearly trampled the manager underfoot when we ran past him like a cattle stampede. If we do, we will have to admit what happened and he will laugh his head off." Alan shook his head sorrowfully and replied, "No, you're right John. We can't go back in again now."

We then pulled up our coat collars and plodded off into the torrential, lashing rain.

A Whole Load of Old Tosh

In the seventies, there arose a confusing situation at Partick Police Office. The two inspectors on my shift both had exactly the same name; John Thompson. This made it confusing when talking about them, particularly as both inspectors were normally on duty at the same time.

One of the inspectors was a tall, imposing man, well over six foot in height. The other one was, to put it bluntly, short. The only way he could have stretched himself up to the minimum height regulations was to have stood up on the tips of his toes in a pair of ballet pumps.

It was therefore inevitable that, with a very noticeable disparity in their respective heights, they would be called large Inspector Thompson and small Inspector Thompson; later shortened to Big Tosh and Wee Tosh.

Although nobody ever used their titles in front of them, the two inspectors very soon became aware of their nicknames.

Big Tosh was quite happy with his moniker, as he felt that he was described as someone large and strong. Wee Tosh on the other hand was not nearly as pleased with his nickname. He felt that he sounded small and insignificant by comparison.

He was desperate to catch someone referring to him as Wee Tosh so that he could hand out an old fashioned rollicking and make an example of him. However, his chances of catching anyone calling him Wee Tosh were extremely slim.

One evening, he was on duty within Partick Police Office when the telephone rang. He picked up the telephone and said "Partick Police Office here. Can I help you?"

It was one of the late shift cops who asked if he could speak to Inspector Thompson. "Now is my chance," thought Wee Tosh and asked the caller quite innocently, "Who do you want to speak to, Big Tosh or Wee Tosh?" The cop replied "I want to speak to Wee Tosh." "Right," said the inspector triumphantly. "This is Wee Tosh speaking. Who am I talking to?" The voice on the telephone replied, "Don't you know who you are speaking to?" "Of course not," said Wee Tosh irritably through gritted teeth. "That's why I am asking you."

"In that case," said the voice, "go take a running jump at yourself." He then quickly slammed the phone down.

Sudden Deaths

One call every police officer dreads is a request to attend at the scene of a sudden death. They are normally sad and melancholy events with distressed and distraught family members struggling to cope with the situation.

However, over the years there have been occasional humorous moments which have lightened the mood.

I was out on patrol with my neighbour Alex on a lovely summer afternoon when we received a call to attend at the scene of a suspected sudden death on my beat in Partick.

Our hearts immediately sank. Oh no, a maniac wielding a samurai sword or a mad bull on the rampage would have been infinitely more welcome.

There was no escape. As we were the beat men responsible, we had to attend, so off we trudged, albeit very reluctantly. We were then briefed about the circumstances.

A building company had telephoned in to report that their night watchman had not arrived to commence his shift at 5 p.m. after his day off. They also stated that he had never been late for work previously, even though he had been employed there for years. They also advised that they had been telephoning him constantly and had received no reply. Suffice to say, they feared the worst.

We arrived at his abode which luckily for us was the ground floor flat. We started off by banging loudly on the door and shouting at the top of our voices through the letter box. This of course had absolutely no effect. We then made our way through the dunny and emerged at the rear of the flat.

We climbed up on dustbins and peered through the bedroom curtains where we observed the deceased lying in bed. We made sure that he was definitely dead by banging on the windows and shouting loudly, but of course we got absolutely no response.

We then radioed in, confirming that this was a sudden death situation and were instructed to force open the front door. The door was extremely strong and sturdy, and it took some time before we managed to enter the flat.

We made our way through to the bedroom to inspect the body for any suspicious circumstances, or alternatively to confirm that the death appeared to occur from natural causes.

I said to Alex, "We should check his pulse in case he is deeply unconscious and not dead." "Aye, that will be right," said Alex. "You mean *you* will check his pulse. This is your beat, so it is down to you."

Apprehensively, I approached the body. I really did not want to touch the corpse, but I knew that I needed to confirm that this was indeed a death.

Reluctantly, I felt his wrist for a pulse when all hell broke loose. The apparently dead man suddenly sat up and began bellowing at the top of his voice, "My Goad, it's the polis! You frightened the life out of me, so you did. What the hell are you doing in my bedroom?"

I replied, "Calm down. Believe me, you frightened us a lot more than we scared you. We might have to go home for a change of underwear, as we were absolutely certain that you were dead."

We then told him about the telephone calls, the banging on his door, shouting through his letter box, knocking on his bedroom window and finally crashing in his front door, all of which he had slept through.

He was now looking extremely sheepish and embarrassed and asked us what the time was. We told him that it was now after six o'clock and that he should have reported for work at 5 p.m.

"Oh no!" he wailed. "I've slept all night and all day and I'll probably get the sack intae the bargain."

I assured him that, as he was a model employee, his employers were very concerned about his wellbeing. I then asked him how he could possibly have slept through the tremendous racket that we had made before we forced the door.

He explained that Saturday was his only day off each week. He always went to his local pub for a few pints and picked out four horses from the racing section of his newspaper that were being shown on television that afternoon.

He would place a bet at the bookmakers known as a Yankee. It consisted of six cross two bob doubles, four cross two bob trebles and a two bob accumulator. This came to the princely sum of twenty-two shillings, or in decimal money, £1.10p.

He would then return to his house and watch the races on his television. Normally speaking, his bet went down the Swanny without a trace. As he liked to choose outsiders at large odds against, he very rarely managed to pick any winners.

However, on this particular Saturday, to his total astonishment and complete and utter joy, all four of his selections trotted home in first place. He then returned to the bookies and collected his considerable winnings.

After that, he went to the pub and proceeded to drink much more than was normal for him. At the end of the evening, he was still feeling flushed with success, so he bought himself a bottle of whisky for a nightcap.

He then returned home where he poured himself several large ones. Finally, he staggered through to his bed in a highly intoxicated and inebriated condition and slept like the dead (the dead drunk, that is).

Again, he became very agitated and anxious about his job and asked me what he could possibly tell his employers to prevent him from getting the sack.

I told him to calm down, have a seat and relax and that I would sort it out for him. I lifted his phone, contacted his employers and advised them of the situation. I mollified them by telling them how upset and embarrassed their employee was for failing to turn up for his shift for the first and only time.

They were so delighted and relieved that he was still alive and well, when they had been convinced that he was deceased, that they gave him the night off and told him to report for duty the following day.

We were all extremely happy and relieved. I was also spared from submitting a long, time-consuming sudden death report.

Sudden Death 2

On another occasion, I attended at a sudden death on my beat. This time unfortunately, it was indeed a death of the sudden variety. The circumstances were as follows:

Two brothers in their sixties had lived together in the family home for their entire lifetimes. Neither of them had married and their parents had passed on some years before, having bequeathed the home equally between both siblings.

The family home, I should add at this point, was a single end in Partick with just one bedroom. The brothers were hard workers and had been regularly employed for many years. They had shared a double bed in the bedroom since birth. However, they had different sleep patterns.

One brother retired to bed at 9 p.m. and rose at 5 a.m. for work, while the other one retired at 11 p.m. and rose at 7 a.m.

On this particular day, the early shift brother had returned from work to discover that his sibling had passed away peacefully in his sleep, exactly how he had left him that morning.

I was instructed to attend at the house to carry out a sudden death enquiry and submit a report regarding the facts and circumstances.

I set the wheels in motion by calling out the family doctor for the deceased. Although he was absolutely certain that the man had died from natural causes, the doctor declined to issue a death certificate, as he was unsure regarding the actual cause of death.

This meant that I was now obliged to call out the police surgeon to have him issue a death certificate. I could then make arrangements to have the body removed and taken to the city mortuary for the purposes of a post mortem.

However, the police surgeon was extremely busy and I was advised that it would be several hours before he could attend to issue the certificate.

He did eventually arrive and completed the essential paperwork, then told me that I could now make arrangements to have the body removed. I contacted the company concerned and arranged for the body to be uplifted and conveyed to the mortuary for post mortem. Unfortunately, they were too busy and could not attend for some time.

As the evening wore on, I observed that the early shift brother was getting more and more agitated and anxious. Eventually, he could contain himself no longer. He blurted out, "Look, I'm sorry big yin, but it's well past my bed time and I'm working in the morning, so I'll need tae get some sleep."

Rather naively, I replied, "Of course, it's getting late. On you go." I had of course forgotten that I was in a single end with only one bedroom. Within one minute, he removed his clothes, put on his pyjamas and leapt into bed beside his dead brother.

I was both horrified and amazed by his actions. In fact, I stood open-mouthed, gaping at him in complete and utter disbelief. My mind was racing frantically as I tried to work out which particular law or by-law he was in contravention of. Fortunately, I couldn't think of any laws, by-laws, rules or regulations that he was breaking, so I finally croaked out, "I'll bid you goodnight then." I closed the bedroom door behind me and returned to the living room.

About one hour later, the undertakers arrived to collect the body. They carried in the lightweight coffin and asked me to take them to the body.

I opened the bedroom door and switched on the light. Of course, by this time, the live brother was deeply asleep and did not stir a muscle. I looked across at the undertakers. Their faces were a study of amazement, incredulity and shock. After a few seconds, one of the men blurted out, "We didnae know there were two of them. We only hae room for one."

I was just about to explain to them that there was only one body when the live brother woke up and sat bolt upright in bed.

The undertakers screamed at the top of their voices and almost knocked me over as they tried to scramble past me to get out of the bedroom. I held the door shut and prevented them from getting out, although it was difficult as they were desperate to escape.

"Calm down" I said. "There is only one body. The other one is his brother who has a very early start in the morning and really needs his sleep."

"Oh, my God," gasped the older undertaker. "I have never seen anything like this before in my life."

"You are absolutely right," I replied, trying my best to keep a straight face and failing miserably. "Neither have I, but at least I knew that one of them was still alive and kicking."

The undertakers then removed the body and set off for the city mortuary. I then wished the live brother a good night's sleep and made my way back to the police office. There, I typed up a sudden death report, regarding all of the pertinent facts and circumstances.

Needless to say, I did not include the part that his brother had played, nor the fright suffered by the undertakers. Some things are better kept to one's self.

I Predict a Riot

I t was Scottish football's Cup Final day at Hampden Park Stadium on a bright, sunny Saturday afternoon.

The draw had worked out perfectly for both the Scottish Football Association and the teeming thousands of football fans attending at the game.

The Old Firm, Rangers and Celtic were appearing against each other in the final, much to everyone's delight.

On that particular day, the Marine Division had drawn the short straw. We were patrolling the perimeter track around the football pitch. On the terracing, we could watch the crowd and the match at the same time. However, our instructions were to keep our eyes entirely on the crowd and ignore the football match taking place beside us.

As we were all fans of one or other of the Old Firm, that was quite a difficult order to follow. Most of us had developed a crick in the neck by the end of the match.

It was nearing the end of the ninety minutes and the game was perfectly poised with both teams level.

The young police officer walking immediately in front of me was a Rangers fanatic. He lived, breathed and dreamed about the team. His best friend at that time was Alex Miller who went on to manage Hibs, and is at present assistant manager at Liverpool Football Club.

At the time of this tale, Alex was a promising young fullback at Rangers, but was not yet a first team regular, so this was obviously a very long time ago.

We were patrolling past the Celtic side when it happened. Rangers broke out after a sustained spell of pressure from Celtic and scored a peach of a goal. (Well, if you were a Rangers supporter, it was a peach of a goal).

Peter leapt up about three feet, taking his police hat off and throwing it skywards. He then performed what can only be described as a joyous jig of pure unadulterated delight. His arms were up in the air and he was shouting, "Ya beauty, yes, yes, yes. Oh, ya beauty."

This performance was taking place immediately in front of the massed ranks of Celtic supporters, "The Bhoys". They very obviously did not agree with Peter about the beauty of the goal. Their initial stunned silence became a snarl, then a growl and finally burst out in to a deafening roar of unbridled rage at the cheek and effrontery of a supposedly unbiased (aye, right) police officer in full uniform appearing to goad them in this manner.

Peter, of course, was completely oblivious about the effects that his unrestrained, deliriously happy celebrations were having on the opposing supporters.

Thousands of them appeared to be moving forward, ready to tear Peter apart, limb from limb. Luckily for him, and for me, the superintendent in charge of our division grabbed Peter and led him up the tunnel and out of sight of the Celtic supporters.

This had the required effect of quietening down the massed crowds of upset and irate Bhoys.

Needless to say, Peter was banned sine die from attending football matches on duty in uniform.

On all occasions thereafter, when the rest of our shift was on duty at a football match, Peter could be seen looking a sad and forlorn sight as he plodded round the beat instead.

My Fair Weather Friend

I reported for the late shift duty on a Sunday afternoon which we all detested because it was usually the longest, most boring shift possible.

Nothing much ever happened on a Sunday and it was quite common to spend the nine hours from 2 p.m. until 11 p.m. without receiving a call of any kind to deal with. In those far-off days we always teamed up with the beat officer from the adjoining beat and on this particular Sunday my neighbour was Mr Magoo.

We were out patrolling our beat and as usual, the streets were absolutely quiet and empty. We had been requested by a pub manager to call in at afternoon closing time and assist him to empty his premises. Eugine, the pub manager was an exuberant, jovial Irishman with lots of Irish customers who were always very reluctant to go home.

We were happy to attend and help out Eugine, as it would break up a long, dreary Sunday afternoon, and also we were guaranteed a pint for our assistance. We arrived at closing time and coaxed and cajoled his reluctant customers to leave the pub.

Eugine thanked us for our help and poured us both a drink. While we were enjoying our pint, we had a convivial chat with Eugine. He then requested a song from me before we left. I was well aware that Eugine loved Irish songs and got quite misty eyed and nostalgic when he heard one.

I was happy to oblige and began singing "If You Ever Go Across The Sea To Ireland." This had exactly the desired effect on Eugine. He immediately lifted our glasses and began refilling them. "Ah, you're a lovely chanter John lad. Give me another one," quoth Eugine. "No problem," I replied and started off another Irish song, "Where The Mountains Of Mourne Sweep Down To The Sea."

Unfortunately for Eugine, Magoo and I received a call from the section sergeant asking us for our position.

I answered the personal radio and gave our position as a few streets away from the pub (after all, we didn't want the sergeant to know exactly where we were).

We then made our way through the back lanes as quickly as possible. We didn't want the sergeant arriving at the position I had given him before we did.

We were in the last back lane, about fifty yards from where we were due to meet up with the sergeant when disaster struck. As we jogged through the lane, Alex did a perfect impersonation of his namesake cartoon character, Mr Magoo.

He tripped over something and did a swallow dive, arms outstretched, sailing through the air with all the grace and poise of an overweight elderly walrus. He then landed with a perfectly executed belly flop in a large muddy puddle. I helped him up, but he was covered in mud from head to toe. He really lived up to his nickname because his spectacles were coated in mud and he couldn't see a thing.

Fortunately, help was at hand. Further along the lane, I could see rainwater gushing out of an overhead gutter, no doubt blocked at the downpipe. I swiftly persuaded Alex to stand under the deluge of water which would hopefully wash the mud from his face, hat, uniform coat and trousers. He very reluctantly did so and managed to wash the mud off, but Magoo was now absolutely soaked. If he had dived into the Clyde and swam over to the other side, (a most unlikely scenario for Magoo) he could not have been any wetter.

We then walked out of the lane and into the street just as the sergeant arrived in his panda car. He stepped out of the vehicle and looked us up and down. His face was a study of perplexed amazement. There I was, standing beside Magoo as dry as a bone, whilst he was dripping water out of every orifice.

Totally baffled by our respective appearances, but not wishing to pry, the sergeant asked us if there was anything doing. "No Sergeant," I replied, looking as though butter wouldn't melt in my mouth. "It's been absolutely quiet all afternoon. The streets are empty and there is not an angry man in sight."

"Okay lads, fair enough," said the sergeant who then signed our notebooks and jumped back into his car. Again, he looked us up and down, then shook his head. He obviously knew that something had happened and that we had pulled some sort of a stroke on him, but he couldn't work out exactly what it was.

Poor old Magoo. It did not rain at all that day, but he had never been wetter in his entire life.

A Dash of Lemonade Please

I was still very young and wet behind the ears at the time this event took place. We had been called into a whisky bonded warehouse regarding a quite trivial complaint; so trivial in fact that I can't remember what it was about.

We were taken through to the private office of the managing director and invited to sit down. He explained the nature of the complaint fairly quickly and we noted the details for attention at a later date.

With the business completed, the conversation moved onto general topics. I had noticed when I entered the office that, on the right side of the room, there was a magnificent wooden table, covered with bottles of the finest whisky known to man. Most of the bottles were half to three-quarters full with some still sealed.

The managing director sat back and smiled. "Well, gentlemen," he said. "You cannot come into a whisky bond without sampling our wares." Funnily enough, that was exactly what I was thinking at the time of his comment.

He then went on to wax lyrical about the various types and blends of Scotch whisky on the table. He pointed out each bottle individually and gave a brief history of each brand. Every bottle on the table had been matured in whisky casks for at least fifteen years, with some of the bottles twenty or twenty-five years vintage. There were single malts, double malts and numerous versions of the very finest hand blended whisky.

He eventually finished his narrative and asked us to choose from his highly impressive list. My neighbour asked for a single malt while I opted for a particularly well blended twenty-year-old limited edition. Each and every bottle on display that day would now be worth hundreds of pounds with collector's item status.

The managing director lifted up three ornate, beautifully cut crystal goblets from the table and poured out our choices along with his own. He then asked us if we would like anything in our whisky. My neighbour being much longer in the tooth than me immediately demurred and stated that he wouldn't dream of putting anything into such a fine and rare single malt. I unfortunately still had the country yokel straw growing out of my ears.

I blurted out, "Could I have a dash of lemonade in mine please?" He looked at me incredulously and spluttered, "Certainly Officer. I will just phone through for the company accountant."

A couple of minutes later, the accountant arrived. The managing director and he each produced a key and proceeded to open up the safe. A bottle of lemonade was then produced and I received my requested dash. The accountant then made an official entry in a ledger, also kept within the safe, stating the time and date that the lemonade had been used.

I sat there cringing with embarrassment at my faux pas, although it didn't prevent me from consuming and enjoying my drink. It seemed so bizarre and incongruous that all of the bottles of rare and incredibly expensive whisky sat there on the table for anyone to help themselves to, while the lemonade was carefully locked away in a safe and a record kept of its use.

My neighbour explained to me afterwards that the whisky inside the bonded warehouse had not yet had the astronomical government excise duty imposed on it.

This enormous tax only came into effect when the whisky left the warehouse and went on sale to the general (or should that be gullible?) public. Although it is a fairly lengthy process, whisky is comparatively cheap to produce. Once again, a Scottish industry does all of the hard work and the government rakes off obscene profits from its efforts.

Over the years, I had opportunities to call at the bonded warehouse frequently, but I never again made the mistake of asking for a dash of lemonade.

The Tragic Tale of Tam's Ten Bob Note

B ig Tam was a large, jovial Irishman and had been the office beat man at Cranstonhill Police Office for many years (known as the office beat because the building was right in the centre of his beat area).

I had been out on the beat with Big Tam many times and had seen him performing his party trick on many occasions. It went like this. Either we would see out the customers of a public house at closing time, then stay behind for a few drinks (on the house, of course) or alternatively look in during opening hours and give the staff a nod, which meant we would come back after they had closed for business.

The owner or manager of the pub knew the score and would immediately set up at the very least two free rounds of drinks. On almost all of those visits, Big Tam (who must have kissed the Blarney Stone on many occasions) always managed to charm another round of free drinks with his vast array of jokes and anecdotes.

However, if this failed to work, Tam would play his trump card. He would reach into his inside pocket and pull out his wallet. Inside his wallet was a neatly folded ten shilling note in pristine condition (fifty pence worth in new money).

The next part went like this. He would produce the ten shilling note and state, "My good man. Allow me to buy yourself and your staff a drink before we go." (Remember, we are talking about the early sixties when ten bob would have purchased a number of drinks).

This always resulted in the owner/manager saying, "Don't be silly Tam. Put that away and have another one on me, but thanks for the offer anyway." Tam would then return his wallet to his pocket with a theatrical gesture. This had been a very successful ploy for years, as all the cops at Cranstonhill knew about Big Tam's ten bob note.

However, on the fateful night in question when Tam and I entered one of his favourite establishments, there was a new temporary manager standing in for the regular man who was on holiday.

He set up a round of drinks for us, then instead of listening to Big Tam's patter, he began tallying up the evening's takings and left us to it. Big Tam's other speciality was downing his first pint of Guinness in a oner (what else would you expect an Irishman to drink?). All of the regular managers knew this and would pour Tam's second pint for him to enjoy at his leisure straight after handing him his first pint.

Very quickly, Tam downed his first pint and was ready for another. However, the temporary manager did not appear to know the score and failed to offer Tam his second round of drinks.

In desperation, Tam decided to play his trump card and produced the ten bob note and as usual announced, "My good man. Allow me to buy yourself and your staff a drink."

Big Tam was feeling confident. After all, he had worked his party piece hundreds of times before. Then suddenly, disaster struck. The temporary manager reached over and deftly removed the brand spanking new ten shilling note from Tam's hand.

Big Tam's face was a mixture of emotions; incredulity, astonishment, sheer horror, followed by total amazement. His jaw dropped open and for probably the first time in his life, he was completely and utterly speechless.

The manager then really rubbed salt in the wound by telling Tam, "That will be another seven and sixpence please Officer." Tam rummaged through his pockets, finally producing a large handful of loose change to make up the extra cost of the round.

I tried very hard to keep a straight face, but found it impossible to refrain from chuckling when I looked at the expression on Big Tam's face. He was completely devastated and looked a broken man.

Tam was so shocked by the whole experience, he forgot to ask me to go halves. It was an unwritten rule that if the unthinkable ever happened and a publican ever accepted money from a cop, his partner would pay for half the cost of the round.

In practice, this just didn't ever happen, which was why Big Tam was so completely gobsmacked by this unfortunate turn of events. Of course, I never ever did remind him of the fact that I should have donated my half.

Escort Duty

I t was a midweek early shift morning and I was on plainclothes patrol duty. As absolutely nothing was happening to occupy our attention, the time was passing exceedingly slowly.

Then right out of the blue, we received a message on our personal radio to meet up with the divisional car which would convey us directly to Partick Police Office.

We arrived at the police office and liaised with the shift inspector. He informed us that he had been contacted by Ipswich Police Force who had a notorious Glasgow criminal in custody.

They had checked him out on the police national computer and discovered that he was wanted on several arrest warrants in Glasgow. The most important warrant was for Partick Police Office. They requested that two officers from Partick travel down to Ipswich with the warrant and escort him back.

The inspector asked us if we would like to do the escort duty which would entail us staying overnight in Ipswich and escorting the prisoner back the following day by train to Glasgow Central Station.

Do bears shit in the woods? "Yes sir, please sir, three bags full sir." To be fair, if this proposition of an available overnight escort duty had been put to the entire shift at

6.45 a.m. when we commenced early shift duty, every hand would have shot up.

We all liked escort duty that entailed an overnight stay for two reasons. (1) In the words of Arthur Daley (George Cole) from the television series Minder, it was a nice little earner; hours of overtime plus overnight expenses called subsistence payments. (2) It was a complete change of scenery, and a good night out was guaranteed with the local C.I.D.

The reciprocal arrangements were that if English police officers came to Glasgow on an overnight escort duty, our C.I.D. took them out for a few drinks in the evening. It did of course work vice versa when we travelled down to England.

The regular plainclothes officers were always given first refusal for those duties. There would have to be something exceptionally important happening at home that evening to turn it down, and we certainly didn't even consider doing that.

The divisional car drove us home where we each collected an overnight bag of pyjamas, underwear, toothbrush etc. I should explain that my plainclothes partner Willie and I were the regular plainclothes men at Partick for several years together. We were known far and wide as Charlie Farley and Piggy Malone. Just our luck to be on plainclothes duty at the same time the Two Ronnies was the biggest show on television. At that time, they played the hapless comedy detectives of those names.

The top crooks in Glasgow must have been in a state of fear and alarm at the thought of Charlie Farley and Piggy Malone on their case.

However, to return to the story, we boarded the train for Ipswich, armed with the arrest warrant for the prisoner. The journey south was lengthy, but we had come prepared by bringing a pocket set of chess with us. Willie and I considered ourselves intellectual giants of the chessboard. Aye, right, but it passed the time.

We arrived at Ipswich where we were met by the local C.I.D. car and taken to the police office where we completed all the paperwork formalities with the officer-on-duty.

He then advised us to introduce ourselves at the police guest house, which was part of the same building, and deposit our overnight bags. Once there, we washed and brushed up before returning bright eyed and bushy tailed to meet up with our English colleagues.

They suggested that we go for a pint before we ate. We of course agreed as we wanted to co-operate with the local police force, even though we would have preferred to have spent a quiet night in, drinking tea and watching Coronation Street.

We arrived at the first pub where we immediately offered to buy the first round. We were told that we were their guests and to put our money away.

The C.I.D. officers obviously knew the owner of the pub well. They introduced us as the crime fighting cops from Glasgow who had arrived to take the infamous villain who had been terrorising the pubs of Ipswich back up to Glasgow to face the music.

This of course had the desired effect with the publican, shaking our hands, thanking us and insisting that the drinks were on the house.

After a while, we moved on to another pub where exactly the same circumstances took place; profuse thanks followed by free drinks, and at the next pub, and the one after that, and again at the next one.

Eventually, all of the pubs were closed and we assumed that we would now go for something to eat, but that still was not on the agenda.

Instead, we arrived at a nightclub where predictably, we were once again introduced as the shining white knights from Glasgow who were taking Mr Big back up there with them.

Once again, drinks on the house were forced upon us, despite our admittedly feeble, lacklustre efforts to pay for a round. We were halfway through our pint when I glanced over to the dance floor at the club patrons.

I slowly became aware that something wasn't quite right, but what was it? I gulped in amazement when I realised what it was; all of the dancers were men.

To say that I was surprised was a complete understatement. I had never seen anything like it before. After all, this was in the late sixties or early seventies. The local C.I.D. officers were watching us slyly, waiting for us to notice. They grinned broadly when they observed the astonished looks on our faces.

Almost half of the club patrons were dressed as women and I do mean the full bhoona; dresses, tights, wigs, high heeled shoes, lipstick, mascara, the works. Unfortunately, they didn't possess the natural rhythm and grace of ladies. In fact, on closer inspection, they danced more like pantomime dames. Quite obviously, they didn't wear high heels on a daily basis and were a bit unsteady on them.

At this point, two of the ladies (did I just say ladies?) tottered over to our table and made straight for Willie and me. The first lady looked like Desperate Dan in drag, built like a brick shithouse and he obviously hadn't shaved for several days.

The conversation went like this. First lady: "It's nice to see some fresh young blood in the club. Would you like to dance?" Willie and I both hesitated. We certainly weren't going to dance, but we didn't want to be rude and tell them to go away and leave us alone.

This hesitation allowed the second lady to add, "Come on boys. Get on the dance floor and trip the light fantastic." I decided to be diplomatic and said, "Thank you so much for your kind invitation, ladies," (note how I called them ladies) "but we don't dance. Thank you for asking us."

The two ladies (there I go again. Get a grip) burst into peals of laughter, as did our C.I.D. companions. Willie and I joined in as it was now abundantly clear that we had been set up.

After another round of drinks, we were ready to move on. I had noticed that there was only one normal young lady in the club; the waitress serving us our drinks. She was displaying an impressive cleavage in a low cut dress. I remarked to the detective beside me that I was surprised at an attractive young lady working in a club catering for gay men.

He smiled and winked at me, then whispered, "Don't you believe it John. One of our young single cops walked her home and discovered to his horror that she still has a full set of meat and two veg downstairs."

We left the club shortly after 2 a.m. and by this time, Willie and I were absolutely starving, although we didn't give much for our chances of getting something to eat at this late hour.

However, our colleagues seemed quite optimistic about finding somewhere to eat, even this late. They asked us if we liked Indian food. We replied, "Do penguins like fish? You bet we do."

We duly arrived at a large Indian restaurant, but it was completely in darkness, locked up for the night. "Never mind, let's check out the back," said one of our colleagues. Sure enough, there were lights on in the kitchen and the owner and two of his staff were preparing for the following night's business.

We were introduced to the owner and he was advised that we were the two most dynamic fearless crime fighting cops in Glasgow and that we were taking the local villain back up there in the morning. He was absolutely delighted, as he had also had problems with him recently.

He was even more pleased when he discovered that we knew his cousin who owned an Indian restaurant in Gibson Street very well and spoke to him regularly. (He was very generous with free curries).

Willie and I offered to foot the bill for the curries, but the owner simply wouldn't consider it.

He said, "You are doing me a great favour taking Mr Big back to Glasgow. He has given me plenty of trouble recently. Be sure to pass on my best wishes to my cousin when you return."

I replied "Of course we will," knowing full well that our message to his relative meant more free curries in Glasgow when we returned.

He then forced free drinks on us while he prepared massive curries. Once again, I offered to pay for the drinks, but he replied that it would be an insult to himself and his family in Glasgow to accept money from me. Far be it from me to upset an entire family by forcing money on them, (aye, right) so I once again put my cash back in my pocket.

Eventually, we left and made our way back to the police guest house. The C.I.D. officers assured us that we would be wakened in the morning in plenty of time to shower, dress and have breakfast before our trip back to Glasgow with Mr Big. We thanked them and retired to bed, falling asleep as soon as our heads touched the pillows.

I was awakened in the morning, although it felt like five minutes later, by one of my English colleagues. I fancied heading to the dining room for a full English breakfast. He grinned and said, "I don't think your mate is having breakfast," before walking away away and smiling to himself.

I strolled through to the shower room and saw that Willie was suffering from vomitas eruption (Latin expression for extreme hangover with severe sickness). He was on his knees in the praying position in front of the toilet bowl; his complexion a delicate shade of green.

I tried to keep a straight face and asked him if he would like me to order him a full English breakfast along with my own. He stared at me incredulously before groaning, "No-oh-oh-oh-oh." I decided not to ask him again as he seemed quite positive about it.

We showered and dressed and made our way to the dining room. Poor Willie, his face was now the palest of pure white porcelain as he gingerly sat down beside me. Almost immediately, an enormous full English breakfast was placed in front of me. This produced an audible groan from Willie who requested a pot of black coffee, but absolutely no food please.

I tucked in with gusto and relish while Willie grimaced at every mouthful. After breakfast, we attended at the police office where we collected Mr Big. We were then driven to the railway station in a police car and escorted onto the train by the local police officers.

We duly arrived back at Glasgow Central Station where we were met by the divisional driver who drove us back to Partick Police Office.

We then completed the paperwork and deposited Mr Big in a police cell. The shift inspector asked us how our trip had gone. I replied, "Extremely quiet sir, a cup of Ovaltine and straight to bed."

He gave us a quizzical look and replied, "That's exactly what I expected from two of my most diligent officers." He then grinned broadly and offered an extremely knowing wink.

The Bacardi Boat

On the occasion of the Bacardi boat, I was on duty in Yorkhill Dock which is immediately adjacent to Queen's Dock (the S. E. C. C. is now situated at this locus. How times have changed). I always found it strange that enormous transporter cargo ships were always referred to as boats and not ships.

I was once again on late shift and my duties were to liaise with senior customs officers along with my neighbour. We were to be briefed on a joint customs and police operation.

We were intrigued to find out what this duty was. As customs officers were involved, we of course knew that it almost certainly involved excisable liquor. We duly arrived and were made aware of the circumstances.

On this occasion, excisable liquor was being brought in to the docks, which made a change as normally, enormous quantities of Scotch whisky were being shipped out. The boat in question contained a large cargo of finest Bacardi white rum. Unfortunately, the ship had run into extremely stormy gale force weather out in the middle of the ocean. The cases of Bacardi had been thrown about in the cargo hold and roughly half of the consignment had been smashed.

The customs officers had decided to write off the entire cargo of Bacardi. This was done by issuing a

Contaminated Goods Order with the ships insurers, covering the full cost of the cargo.

As the entire cargo was written off, this meant that no excise duty would be incurred. The whole cargo was now to be unloaded and destroyed under our joint surveillance.

The Bacardi was duly unloaded into the large dock shed. While half of the consignmemt had been totally smashed, there were also plenty of cases containing undamaged bottles, securely sealed and in pristine condition. I thought to myself, "It's a pity to destroy the undamaged Bacardi. It seems like a dreadful waste."

The customs officers obviously had the same idea as me. The senior officer approached us. He advised us that, as this was a joint customs and police operation, would we please assist them by properly disposing of any undamaged bottles of Bacardi?

His instructions went almost exactly like a sketch from Monty Python. He stated, "I trust you will dispose, wink, wink, nudge, nudge, say no more, of the bottles in a fit and proper manner." He added that all of the bottles must be fully emptied of Bacardi to comply with regulations, wink, wink, nudge, nudge, say no more.

I replied, "Of course we will, customs officer, wink, wink, nudge, nudge, say no more. We will personally see to it that all of the sealed unbroken bottles will be disposed of properly, and that all of the bottles are completely emptied of the contaminated Bacardi, wink, wink, nudge, nudge, say no more."

My neighbour and I decided that this responsible and onerous task was a bit too much for just the two of us. We therefore shared out the unbroken sealed bottles with the rest of the late shift on duty that day. We advised them of the Contaminated Goods Order placed on the cargo by the customs officers. We then gave them strict instructions that the contents of the bottles had to be disposed of in a proper manner and totally emptied, nudge, nudge, wink wink, say no more.

However, even after sharing out the contaminated bottles, we were still left with several each to deal with (a difficult job but somebody had to do it).

By sheer luck, my weekend off was approaching and my in-laws were coming over to stay with us for a couple of days.

I brought home some two litre bottles of Coca Cola, as I had been advised that this was the proper mixer for Bacardi. It was a fairly new import to Scotland and I hadn't tried it yet.

I was anxious to dispose of the Bacardi quickly, so that evening I poured everyone copious quantities of the stuff, topped off with large amounts of Coca Cola.

My young brother-in-law Stewart had recently turned eighteen, but unlike the eighteen year olds of today, he had practically no experience of strong drink. Ah, but tonight he was about to get some.

That evening, I witnessed my first ever experience of projectile vomiting. Stewart was a quiet studious young man, extremely shy and wouldn't say boo to a goose. Now here he was clamouring to sing and he wasn't going to take no for an answer.

I told him that he was next for a song after I had finished singing. I believe at that time I was performing my 27th or perhaps my 28th number (good stuff, that Bacardi and coke).

Then suddenly, Stewart told us that he thought he was going to be sick and made a beeline for the bathroom which was upstairs. I followed him up to make sure that he was all right. He very nearly made it to the bathroom, but unfortunately not quite.

On the top step of our stairway, he exclaimed, "Oh, no," whereupon a jet of vomit shot from his mouth with the speed and velocity of a high pressure fire hose. It almost bored a hole through our freshly wallpapered wall (I had only finished wallpapering the previous day).

The following morning, several of my in-laws had hangovers, with young Stewart suffering the most (he wasn't volunteering to sing now). Even now, some forty years later, I don't believe Stewart has ever again been able to face a Bacardi and coke.

Never mind. At least we disposed of the contaminated Bacardi very quickly and efficiently as per our specific instructions from the customs officers, nudge, nudge, wink, wink, say no more.

The Leopard

This is yet another story from the docks. On this occasion, I was on late shift on dock duty patrol in Meadowside Docks, quite close to Partick Police Office. My neighbour had just left to make his way to the office for his meal break, whilst I was due in for my break one hour later.

I was patrolling the dockside when I met two of the ship's officers returning to their vessel. The ship was from South America, as were the officers. I chatted to them briefly and they invited me aboard for a visit. It was a Sunday afternoon and the docks were completely dead with no dockers, or for that matter, any other tradesmen working that day.

I therefore accepted their offer and was shown in to the captain's cabin. I was then asked if I would like to have a drink with them as their honoured guest. Being mindful of keeping diplomatic relations cordial and friendly, I accepted their kind offer.

We had been chatting sociably for several minutes when I received the biggest fright of my life. Strolling majestically into the cabin came a fully grown adult leopard. For the purposes of this story, it was a leopard (in fact I believe it was actually an ocelot).

The enormous, snarling, ferocious, slavering beast walked straight over to me, placed his huge front paws on my shoulders and opened its mighty jaws to reveal terrifying gleaming white fangs (I sometimes tend to exaggerate a little).

I was on the point of passing out when I noticed that the officers were all grinning just before laughing out loudly. The leopard sniffed me all over and decided that he wasn't quite ready for his next meal. Therefore, he turned around and strolled back out of the cabin.

The officers then told me that they had adopted the orphaned cub when its mother had been killed by hunters in the South American forests. They had brought it back to their ship and hand reared it with a baby's bottle. The leopard had grown up with the crew and they treated it like the ship's cat. It was completely tame and docile and had never been off the ship in its life.

The leopard knew all of the crew, and it was only when a stranger came aboard the ship that the leopard always checked them out in the same fashion by placing his front paws on their shoulders and sniffing them all over.

The officers of course knew exactly what would happen when they invited me aboard their ship and thoroughly enjoyed my discomfort.

Once I had calmed down, I realised that it must have been very funny and amusing to observe my reaction when the big cat's wide open jaws were mere inches from my face.

I then devised, in the words of Baldrick from Blackadder, a cunning plan. I spoke to the officers and they were delighted to assist me.

Later that evening, I met up with my neighbour Eddie who was well known for his love of practical jokes. However, on this occasion, the joke was to be on him. I advised him that the captain had invited us aboard for a social drink with the officers.

Eddie immediately brightened up. He had not been looking forward to several hours of patrolling the deserted docks with only the company of the hundreds of rats that scuttled about in the sheds after it got dark.

We received a visit from the section sergeant who signed our notebooks which then left us clear until we went off duty at 11 p.m.

"I think we should now accept the captain's kind invitation," said I. "You are absolutely right," said Eddie, and we proceeded to board the ship.

We were warmly welcomed in to the captain's cabin as arranged. We were offered a drink by the captain who began pouring his officers and ourselves one. However the bottle was only half full and ran out before all of the drinks had been poured.

The captain then turned round to Eddie and asked him if he wouldn't mind popping in to the cabin next door to bring through another bottle. "No problem captain," said Eddie who strode into the adjoining cabin. However, unfortunately for Eddie, there was more than a bottle waiting for him.

We gave my neighbour a few seconds, then crept through behind him. There stood the petrified Eddie, standing as still as a statue, scarcely daring to breathe. The leopard was doing his usual thing with a stranger; front paws on Eddie's shoulders and sniffing him all over.

We all started laughing uproariously, with me laughing the loudest because I knew exactly how Eddie was feeling. Meanwhile, Eddie was using a few choice phrases to describe me and turning the air blue. He had by now worked out that I had stitched him up like a kipper and was not very happy about it.

We then returned to the captain's cabin, where Eddie was more than ready for a stiff drink and very nearly a change of underpants.

Christmas Night in the Workhouse

I t was Christmas Eve and I was on the night shift. It was the late sixties and in those days, (or to be absolutely accurate, those nights) the night shift ran for six weeks, followed by twelve weeks on days; the early shift one week and back shift the next week. Oh, yes, we had it tough in those days.

I sadly left home and jumped on a bus. In the sixties, police officers in uniform travelled free on the buses and nearly all of the cops used public transport at that time. I arrived at Cranstonhill Police Office and reported for duty.

That evening, I was detailed to cover Queen's Dock from 11 p.m. until 7 a.m. which as I mentioned earlier, was a huge, bustling dockyard in the sixties with merchant ships coming and going on a daily basis from all over the world. There were normally two cops detailed to police the docks. However, as this was Christmas Eve, there were no ships present. I therefore made my sorrowful, sad and lonely way down there all alone.

When there were two of us on duty, we had many ways to pass the time and amuse ourselves. On seeing foreign seamen entering the docks in the late evening and early hours of the morning, we usually approached, stopped and questioned them in the following way.

We advised them that they were entering a restricted area and asked them what their business was here. They would then tell us which ship they were stationed on and we waved them through. However, on most occasions, they were accompanied by young ladies, in which case they did their best to sneak in past us. We of course knew the docks inside out and could always intercept them before they reached their ship. We then asked them who the young ladies were and the reason for taking them aboard their vessel.

We always received the same response. They would look at us indignantly and state that the ladies were their wives and how dare we suggest otherwise. We of course had the advantage of knowing that the young women were Hairy Mary and Saggy Aggie, two of our local ladies of the night. They were part of a large group of young ladies who congregated at Betty's Bar on a nightly basis to pick up foreign seamen and spend the night with them on their ships... for an agreed fee, of course. These working girls were no amateurs.

Of course, we could have replied, "That's strange because you are the third set of husbands those ladies have arrived in the docks with this week alone." However, we kept a straight face and let them through, pretending that we believed them. They were far from the first and certainly not the last sailors to be fleeced by the ladies of the night.

Sadly for me, this was Christmas Eve and there were no sailors or ladies of the night to break up the monotony of a long night patrolling the empty docks.

It was a white Christmas this particular year with a thick covering of snow on the ground. I approached the dock gates, whistling that happy joyful song, "Oh, Lonesome Me." Yes, you could say that I was feeling a little sorry for myself, spending an eight hour night shift alone on this festive evening.

Then I saw it shining out like a beacon on the virgin, unbroken snow; a light on in the harbour master's hut, right next door to the police box. I should mention that this particular police box was not like Doctor Who's Tardis. No, this was a large wooden cabin which contained a spacious sitting/dining room, separate kitchen and toilet. All in all, a regular home from home. The harbour master's office was of a similar size and layout.

Back to the story, I had convinced myself that I would have been the only living creature roaming about the docks all night, except of course for the hundreds of rats scurrying about underfoot and the bats swooping by like ghostly apparitions, in the darkness. To say then that I was both surprised and delighted was an understatement.

As there were no ships in the docks, I had not expected the harbour masters to be out on duty. I entered the police box and made an entry in the box diary that I was in attendance and had commenced my night shift duties.

I then popped next door to see who was on duty and was delighted to find that it was two of the regular harbour masters who I knew quite well. They were both highland gentlemen from the Western Isles, Lachie and Donny, well versed in the art of highland hospitality. They demonstrated this right away saying, "Ah, John lad. We were hoping it would be someone that we knew. You are invited to our Christmas dinner. It will be a black tie do."

"Aye, right," I replied. "It was lucky I came prepared then." This was of course in reference to the fact that black ties were part of both police and harbour master uniforms. I then asked, "What time would you like me to attend for your Christmas dinner?" Donny replied, "Round about 2 a.m. for before-dinner drinks, then dinner at 3 a.m." The harbour masters certainly knew how to arrange a dinner party.

"Good on you, gentlemen," I replied. "That gives me time to do a full patrol of the sheds and check up on the watchmen." The enormous sheds in Queen's Dock were literally packed full to the gunnels with all kinds of luxury brands of export whisky, waiting to be loaded onto the visiting ships. There was a night watchman stationed within every shed and it was part of our night patrol duties to call in to check that the watchmen were all present and correct. All police dock officers had a key to get into each shed. The doors all opened inwards and the watchmen had telltales behind the doors which consisted of metal strips and bars that fell onto the concrete floor when the door was opened from the outside.

This of course caused a loud clanging noise which reverberated through the shed, giving the watchman time to wake up before we reached him, allowing him to look as if he was fully alert and on top of his job when we arrived. We of course tried to catch them out on occasions by opening the door very slowly and putting our hand inside to grab any metal poles.

We would then enter the shed very quietly and make our way to the watchman's quarters. There, we would invariably find them tucked up as snug as a bug in a rug, snoring their heads off.

The next step was to stand right beside them and in a loud, stentorian voice bellow, "How's it going watchie? Is everything ship shape and Bristol fashion?" This usually resulted in the watchman uttering a small shriek of fright before jumping to his feet and attempting to pretend that he hadn't actually been sleeping on the job.

We tried valiantly to keep a straight face at this embarrassment and discomfiture at us catching him out. After a brief chat, we then carried on to the next watchman and did our best to surprise him too.

However, this was Christmas Eve and I had just been invited to Christmas dinner, so I made sure that I knocked over all of the telltales to warn the watchmen that I was on my rounds. Yes, I was absolutely full of the Christmas Spirit, showing goodwill to all men.

About 1.45 a.m., the section sergeant called to sign my notebook and dropped the broad hint that he would be tied up for the rest of the night and that I was now on my own until 7 a.m. when my night shift ended. Exactly what the doctor ordered. I was now free to relax and enjoy my Christmas dinner, and I intended to do just that.

As I shook the snow off, the harbour masters were delighted to welcome me into their office where their fire was glowing brightly. They had really prepared themselves for their Christmas meal. There was a freshly laundered tablecloth on the table and they had brought in some of their best dishes and cutlery from home.

Every so often, when foreign ships arrived at the dock, some of their cargo had been damaged during storms at sea. Part or sometimes all of the damaged cargo was deemed unfit for human consumption by the customs officers. This was placed in a pile to be uplifted and taken off to the rubbish tip. However, there were many dozens of tinned goods with barely perceptible tiny dents in them. On those occasions, the customs men always tipped the wink to the dock police officers and the harbour masters, as we were at the top of the food chain. We then had first pick from the pile before it was thrown open to the other numerous tradesmen within the dock.

If truth be told, it usually finished up with a very small pile left to be taken away and dumped. The harbour masters had been stockpiling the undamaged tins for some time, what with Christmas approaching, and had a veritable feast waiting for me.

They had a small typewriter in their office, with which they had typed up menus for our Christmas dinner. Drinks consisted of tins of lager and beer, a large jug of draught dock sherry donated by customs officers, and two bottles of the finest export whisky (hidden inside a hidey hole by dockers, but discovered by the harbour masters, as I explained in an earlier chapter).

The starter course consisted of four kinds of soup, followed by a main course of roast chicken or beef stew with new potatoes, roast potatoes, sliced carrots, garden peas, mixed diced vegetables, pickled beetroot or pickled gherkins. The dessert was a choice of mixed diced fruit, pineapple chunks, creamed rice, sticky syrup sponge pudding or spotted dick with evaporated milk.

Everything on the menu came of course from a tin, even the chicken. The potatoes were simply parboiled, then roasted in their oven. All in all, it was a menu fit to grace a high class restaurant. I thought long and hard about it and decided that yes, I would dispense with my cheese sandwiches and accept their kind offer to dine with them.

The harbour masters office had a panoramic view of the docks. We could spot anything or anybody entering and could see right down the front of the whisky sheds. The front of the police box was also in view, and the flashing light if the telephone went for me. It was the perfect place to take observations of the dock without actually walking about in the still-falling snow.

We sat down for pre-dinner drinks while we decided on our starter, main course and dessert. I had already chosen the spotted dick as I was extremely partial to having it smothered in evaporated milk. I really liked to look after my cholesterol in those days.

The meal was a roaring success. Good food in agreeable company, washed down with delicious draught dock sherry. There were no calls or incidents to deal with and the dock remained deserted until I phoned off duty via the police box at 7 a.m.

I arrived home at my digs (I was still a single young man in those days). My landlady asked me what I would like for my breakfast and I replied with a perfectly straight face, "Nothing for me, thanks. I had such a busy night that I didn't manage a refreshment break until very late this morning when I had your delicious cheese sandwiches." I didn't have the heart to tell her that the pigeons and the seagulls had scoffed the lot.

New Year's Eve

O ne week later, I was again on night shift, but on this occasion I was really looking forward to it. It was now New Year's Eve, or to be proper and correct in Scotland, it was of course, Hogmanay.

Exactly one week before, I had been dreading spending eight long, lonely hours in a deserted dock on my own, and just look how that turned out. Tonight, my beat was up in Charing Cross, the centre of all nightlife in the West End of Glasgow.

I knew that my neighbour and I would be kept busy for the first few hours with the throngs of crowds milling around the area. I also knew that we had been invited to call in to several of our watering holes in the wee small hours of the morning, as they would be on the go long after their normal times.

I had even worked out my repertoire of songs when I would be cajoled, albeit very reluctantly, in to giving them a song (aye, right. Try and hold me back). In some establishments it would be sentimental Irish songs, in others, traditional Scottish or tear jerking ballads. I knew exactly what was appropriate for each one.

Oh, yes, I was ready, willing and able for the night ahead as I stepped jauntily into Cranstonhill Police Office to be given my beat duties for that night. However, within thirty seconds, all of my hopes and plans for the night ahead came crashing down around me.

The section sergeant approached me saying, "Oh, good John. I'm glad you are sharp." I was in fifteen minutes early for reporting on duty. He then said, "You know that you are on beat until seven tomorrow morning." I replied "Of course sarge." Mentally, I was thinking, "Yah beauty. Thank goodness." I was worried that he might have changed my beat and ruined all of my plans.

His next sentence hit me like a ton of bricks. "The alarm is in operation at the supermarket on your beat on Great Western Road and all of the registered keyholders are away on holiday. We won't be able to contact an emergency keyholder until after nine a.m. tomorrow morning, so I'm afraid that you are going to have to stand by it all night. Could you just make your way up there now and relieve the back shift beat man, as he has been standing by since six o'clock tonight and he must be thoroughly fed up." "How right you are, sarge," I replied. "I know exactly how he must be feeling."

As it was pouring with rain and blowing a gale, I secured my hat on my head with the chin strap and set off grimly to relieve the back shift beat man. I arrived at the supermarket and saw him standing forlornly at the main entrance. He spotted me approaching and his face lit up like a beacon. I had seldom seen anyone looking so happy to see me. I, on the other hand, was looking so down in the mouth that I almost stood on my bottom lip.

"Am I glad to see you?" he said. "Yeh, I had noticed," I muttered grimly through gritted teeth. He then shook my hand and wished me a happy New Year when it comes.

He practically knocked me over as he then rushed past me to go off duty and enjoy his Hogmanay.

I buttoned my top coat button against my chin, as no matter where I stood, the wind and heavy rain was lashing around me and trickling down under my shirt collar. The bustling crowds were getting fewer as they battled through the elements to get home for the bells.

I felt as if I had been standing there for days, although I had only been there for one hour when the church bells and ships' horns heralded in the New Year. It was the first and the only time that I had seen the New Year in entirely on my own. Oh, yes, I was feeling sorry for myself. After all, I had been looking forward to my night shift that night. Now here I was, stuck out in the howling wind and torrential rain for eight long agonising hours.

About ten past twelve, a couple of wee Glasgow punters staggered unsteadily past me. One of them looked over and spotted me standing at the front door of the shop. He roared over to me, "Haw big yin, a happy New Year to you." I tried to summon up a smile, but failed miserably. "Thank you," I replied. "And a happy New Year to you too."

The interminable night went on and on for what seemed like days, then weeks, then months (as you know, I am prone to exaggerate at times). Eventually, seven o'clock in the morning arrived. Time for my long, mournful shift to end.

At last, I saw the early shift beat man approaching to relieve me from my standing by duties. I now knew exactly how the late shift beat man felt when he saw me approaching; something akin to pure, unbridled joy. For the first time in eight long, uncomfortable, weary hours, I was grinning like a Cheshire cat. He on the other hand did not look very happy to see me.

I extended my hand and wished him a happy New Year. "Aye, right" he said. "And the same to you. I had great plans for today. Places to go and people to see." "I know just how you feel," I replied. "I had precisely the same plans when I started my night shift eight hours ago." "Anyway," I continued. "I can't stand here all morning chatting. I have a warm bed waiting for me."

"Aye, rub it in, why don't you?" he growled, and without further ado, I was off, leaving him to curse his misfortune, just as I had many hours before.

I arrived back at my digs cold and wet, but extremely happy to be off duty at last. My landlady greeted me in the hall, wishing me a happy New Year. She then said, "I suppose you will be going straight to bed, just like you did last week." "On the contrary, my dear lady," I replied. "This morning, I will have sausage, bacon, black pudding, mushrooms, potato scones, tomato and eggs."

She chuckled and said, "My goodness, that's quite a change. Last week, you were absolutely stuffed." "Yes, I know," I responded wearily, "but last week and last night could not have been more different."

A short time later, I sat down in front of a huge fry up and devoured it like a man who hadn't seen food for a week. I then tumbled into bed and thought about both shifts and how much I had looked forward to last night's duty, only to have all of my hopes and dreams cruelly dashed before I had even started. "Yes" I thought. "Rabbie (Robert Burns) had it completely right when he wrote, "The best-laid plans of mice and men gang aft aglay."

Skip Lady

T his is a tale of my time in the Support Unit. On this Saturday morning, we were on patrol in a Support Unit van in Glasgow city centre. Our group consisted of a driver and six officers in uniform within the vehicle.

Our main purpose later that afternoon was to patrol outside Parkhead Football Stadium. There was an Old Firm football match scheduled to take place between the ancient football rivals Celtic and Rangers. This of course meant that there was a strong likelihood of fights, general disorder and all kinds of breaches of the peace.

However, this was early morning and the streets were deserted and empty. It was in fact the lull before the storm, as several hours later these same streets would be a heaving, throbbing mass of football supporters making their way to the big match.

We were driving slowly past one of the very well known public houses in the East End, close to the site of Glasgow's famous Barra's Market. Then it happened. A Glasgow Worthy walked out of a back court and began waving frantically at us to stop the police vehicle.

We stopped and listened to what he wanted to tell us. He was in a very obviously frightened and shaken up state. The words came tumbling from his mouth at breakneck speed.

In typical Stanley Baxter parliamo Glasgow, he stated "AFUNDTHEBOADYOAWUMMINAHINTTHEDU NNYINASKIP." Luckily enough, we all understood parliamo Glasgow. The man was informing us that he had found the body of a woman behind the exit from the basement of the rear tenement close in a skip.

He then became very defensive and protested his innocence. "It was nothing to do with me," he said. "I was only looking in the skip to see if there was anything worth having. The last thing I expected to see was a dead body."

We assured him that we were treating him as a very important witness, as he had potentially discovered the body of a murder victim. We then left him in the van with the driver who was noting down his particulars.

The accepted practice when a number of police personnel attended at a crime or major incident was that the first officer at the scene became the officer-in-charge and was responsible for all of the often lengthy reports required. A murder was right at the top of the pile and would result in masses of paperwork.

I was seated right at the back of the police vehicle and was accordingly the last one out of the van. The six of us then made our way round to the back court to check out the skip.

As we approached, my five colleagues in front of me did their own version of the Michael Jackson Moon Walk. Although they appeared to be walking forwards, they were actually walking backwards.

This meant that, although I was last out of the police van and walking slowly, I still reached the skip first, automatically becoming the officer-in-charge.

I tentatively peered over the edge of the skip and my heart sank when I observed the body of a woman. She was naked from the waist down, lying on top of a pile of rubbish.

I turned to my colleagues (who were approaching the skip at the pace of a snail on Mogadon) and informed them that the witness was correct. There was indeed the body of a woman in the skip.

I looked back over the side of the skip and nearly fainted with shock when the corpse opened one eye and looked at me. I don't know who got the greatest surprise, her or me.

She then opened her other eye and said, "Thank Goad, it's the polis. Gonnae hep me oot oh this stinking skip, son?"

I quickly regained my composure and answered her. "Of course madam. We will get you out of it right away." By this time, my extraordinarily slow moving colleagues had reached the skip. Emboldened by hearing me speak to the supposed dead body, they all looked over the edge of the skip together.

The woman shrieked and exclaimed, "Oh my Goad, there's hunners oh them." I thought to myself, "That's a bit of an exaggeration. There's only six of us, after all." She turned round to me, assuming correctly that I was in charge, then asked me if we would all turn our backs for a minute until she had put her knickers on.

"Of course madam," I replied, treating her like a lady, although I strongly suspected that she was not one (spending the night on a pile of smelly rubbish in a skip was a good clue).

A minute later, she called out, "Okay son, that's me respectable. Are yeese gonnae help me oot noo?"

Two of us had to very reluctantly climb into the skip, as every time she stood up, she fell down again. This was due to both the slippery rubbish on the floor of the skip and her inebriation from the night before.

With much huffing and puffing, we managed to lift her up the side of the skip where my colleagues then succeeded in pulling her out. I then made a very swift exit from the nauseating stench of the contents of the skip and began interviewing the woman.

"What exactly happened?" I asked her. "How did you come to be trapped in a skip overnight." She replied, "That dirty wee bugger Shuggy helped me into the skip, so that we could hae a quicky, so he did, but he widnae help me oot efter it. I wis stuck in it a night, so ah wis."

My colleagues were manfully trying to keep their faces straight, but were failing miserably, snorting and grunting and endeavouring to contain their mirth by putting their hands over their mouths in a vain bid to contain their laughter.

I continued my interview by asking her if she wished to report a complaint of rape or sexual assault against the man concerned.

"Oh, good hivvens no," she replied. "Wee Shuggy bought me a couple of drinks before closing time in the pub, so he was entitled tae a wee shot in the swings so he wis," (Parliamo Glasgow for sex between consenting adults) "but" she added angrily, "he should hive helped me oot o the skip efter he had his wicked way wi me." By this time, my five colleagues could no longer contain their mirth.

They were now laughing uproariously, walking back towards the van and leaving me with her. Trying my utmost to keep my face straight, I asked her if she was satisfied with the police action. "I'm delighted," she replied. "I would still have been lying in that stinking skip if you hadnae arrived. I wis so happy to get oot o there so a wis."

"As was I madam," I responded absolutely truthfully. "As was I."